Time:
The Second Secret

by

Kathryn Andries

For permission, serialization, condensation, adaptions, or for our catalog of other publications, write to Ozark Mountain Publishing, Inc., P.O. Box 754, Huntsville, AR 72740, ATTN: Permissions Department.

Library of Congress Cataloging-in-Publication Data

Time: The Second Secret by Kathryn Andries -1967-

This book challenges our preconceived ideas about time, and serves as a road map for manifesting our desires quickly.

1. Manifestation 2. Spiritual 3. Time 4. Metaphysical
I. Andries, Kathryn, 1967 II. Metaphysical III. Manifestation IV. Title

Library of Congress Catalog Card Number: 2021948074
ISBN: 9781950608232

Cover Art and Layout: Victoria Cooper Art
Book set in: Elina Decor & Times New Roman
Book Design: Summer Garr
Published by:

OZARK
MOUNTAIN
PUBLISHING

PO Box 754, Huntsville, AR 72740
800-935-0045 or 479-738-2348; fax 479-738-2448
WWW.OZARKMT.COM

Printed in the United States of America

Contents

Chapter 1
The Second "Secret"

Time and the heavens came into being at the same
instant, in order that, if they were ever to dissolve,
they might be dissolved together. Such was the mind
and thought of God in the creation of time.

—Socrates

The first secret to manifestation is understanding how our mind works. Many seekers learned to tap their mental powers with techniques such as visualization, but later became disillusioned when their desires didn't manifest. I have worked with many people who felt lost and betrayed by these metaphysical teachings because their "stuff" didn't manifest. I realized the missing key was the lack of understanding of time.

I have been teaching and studying metaphysics for over twenty years and wanted to explore more deeply why there were so many people who practiced metaphysics, yet had trouble manifesting. This book is the culmination of that search. My desire is to help those in despair who are still waiting for their "stuff" to arrive.

It made sense to me that time would play such a large role since it affects every aspect of our lives. It is the often-ignored and less-understood part of the manifestation process.

When our desires do not manifest in our time frame, we respond in several ways. Some of us may give up and abandon our desires. Others may feel they did something wrong in the manifestation process, and blame themselves, leading to an endless repetition of the process. Another possibility is that we convince ourselves that the desire we formed is not in alignment with our highest good, and so we choose something else.

All these reactions can change when we take time into consideration. The techniques and concepts taught in this book can be used along with the law of attraction to create the life of our dreams.

This book begins with a deep-dive exploration of how time is measured, and the difference between time in the physical and spiritual realms. This leads us to confront the paradox of time; time does exist on the physical level, yet it is meaningless when viewed from the spiritual perspective. Since time doesn't constrain our soul, it is possible to transcend time while living in the world. An amazing variety of methods such as meditation, breathwork, and past life regression have helped people move beyond the structure of time to achieve greatness.

Time is a reflection of what is going on inside of ourselves. So if we want to speed up our manifestations, we need to work on ourselves. This involves examining our thoughts and attitudes and assimilating our experiences. Then we can tap our intuition and allow it to guide us so that we don't waste time with people and things that slow us down.

When we open up to our subconscious in this way, we realize time is our best friend and wants us to fulfill our desires. We can use visualization to show our mind exactly what we want. This mental rehearsal can literally save us days, months, and even years in manifesting our desires. Visualization is especially beneficial when it comes to relationships. There is no need for us to spend so much time hoping and wishing for that special someone. We have the tools to create compatible relationships.

We will study six of the universal laws that specifically relate to time. Knowing how these laws work can give us a huge advantage in the manifestation process and the rate of our evolution.

I will show why engaging in service to others will actually benefit us as much as the receiver. Giving puts us in the driver seat and sets everything in motion. I'll also caution everyone to slow down! Although this might seem contrary to our agenda of moving things along, it will actually help us manifest more quickly. I'll teach you how to recognize the tricks of the ego that cause us to rush through life and how to slow down and smell the roses.

Nature can teach us many things about balance and timing. Our exploration of the four seasons will help us get into the flow. When we are out of balance, we can use one of the four elements to readjust our inner clock. Lastly, when we still feel out of sync and our "stuff" isn't manifesting, it may be time to do some preparation. Many of us want to skip vital steps in order to get to our final destination, but that often leaves us frustrated and blocked from getting the very things we want.

Our conscious mind expects things to happen in a certain order. When an event out of sequence occurs, our first reaction may be to freak out! I hope what I share about events happening out of order will help you appreciate the bigger picture and gain a deeper perspective.

I conclude this book with chapters on my two favorite tools for understanding time cycles: numerology and astrology. I will teach you how to use these tools for predictive purposes and taking advantage of the opportunities that each cycle provides. Any doubts about the validity of these intuitive sciences will perhaps be dispelled when I share the success stories of people who triumphed by taking action during advantageous numerological and astrological cycles.

My hope is that after reading this book, we won't be so quick to abandon our desires when they don't manifest quickly. Rather, we will use the concepts in this book to understand why our desires may not be coming to fruition. Then we can apply the techniques to speed things up.

Let's begin the journey together!

Chapter 2
Time Exploration

The two most powerful warriors are patience and time.

—Leo Tolstoy

Time affects every facet of our lives. We live according to time, planning our schedules based on this illusory thing. For eons mystics have pondered what time is and if it really exists. It is something we usually want more of. It is a mystical thing that is always moving. Sometimes it seems to go slow, other times it moves so fast we don't realize it has passed. Time is sometimes our friend and sometimes our foe. In this chapter we will explore what time is, how we measure it, how to use it wisely, and how time is measured differently according to where we are.

We are like a seed that has its own growth cycle.

If we look in nature, we see that every plant has its own cycle of growth. An apple seedling can take from six to ten years to grow into a tree that bears fruit. Meanwhile, a mung bean seed will sprout in two to three days after planting and is mature in ninety to one hundred twenty days. We came into this lifetime with a blueprint for our growth, which indicates when certain events will happen in our lives. We are all different seeds growing at different times and rates. Experiences are like water to a seed, triggering us to expand and grow beyond what we were yesterday.

What is time? Since time is nonphysical, the best we can do is to describe our experience of it. One way to describe time physically is by the rising and setting of the sun. We experience time in the form of nature. We are aware of the seasons changing, and this is one way we can measure the passing of time. We become more aware of time when we are struggling and in pain, or bored and have nothing to focus on. When we are happy and our mind is actively engaged in some form of creativity, or mentally focused on problem solving, then we become less aware of this space called time.

When we are being triggered by some challenging event, this engages our attention so we become aware of time. Triggers are events in our lives that wake us up. They cause us to look at things differently. Triggers cause us to go into crisis mode, where we are forced to look within. Depending on the severity and intensity of the trigger, we have the potential to learn a lot or a little. We need the triggers to wake up because the ego likes complacency and wants to be in control. Triggers move us beyond complacency to a place where we begin to question who we are and what our purpose is in life. The ego doesn't want us to question such things.

The purpose of the space between triggers is to allow us to process the event and then respond. Can you imagine if our life was one trigger after another with no breaks?

Some of us intentionally create a life with many triggers in order to increase our chances of learning and growing. The triggers produce an internal crisis that motivates us to learn a lesson. Triggers can also produce something wonderful, like falling in love. The main idea behind a trigger is that it causes us to reflect and grow. It just happens that most of us require more intense, challenging triggers to wake us up. Meanwhile, some of us create an easy life with few triggers to simply experience the joy of being. A lifetime with many difficult triggers seems to pass more slowly than lifetimes with fewer challenges. This is mainly due to the fact that when we have unpleasant experiences, we can become stuck to the point where it seems time has stood still. On the contrary, when we are having a great time and enjoying pleasant events, time seems to go quickly because there is no resistance to the joyful events.

There is a distinction between physical and spiritual time. Physical time always moves in a linear fashion and is measured by the movement of the sun. Spiritual time is measured by the amount of understanding or wisdom a person gains. We can say that physical time is horizontal, and spiritual time is vertical. We can use the analogy of the cross, with the vertical and horizontal lines crossing. In the center of the cross, where Jesus was crucified, is when we truly transcend physical time, as Jesus did. By gaining wisdom, we move vertically as we add understandings to the soul. Imagine we are moving along in a linear fashion through our life. As soon as we have an experience and gain wisdom as a result, we move up vertically. Each time we do this, we form a cross, blending our physical experience to form an understanding.

Physical age does not always correlate with our spiritual age. A young wise person can be spiritually more mature than an elderly person. We all get excited about a birthday and celebrate the passage of physical time, yet we often do not celebrate the passage of spiritual learning. Perhaps if we placed more emphasis on celebrating spiritual progress, it would stimulate more of us to focus on gaining wisdom from our experiences.

One spiritual community I studied didn't believe in celebrating birthdays, which only reflected the passage of time. Rather, they celebrated when someone had grown spiritually and made a quantum leap in his evolution. This exemplifies the difference between physical time (e.g., the passing of birthdays) and spiritual time (moving up in your soul evolution).

Physical time is like a ladder; stepping up each rung of the ladder moves you through life. Spiritual time is more akin to throwing a pebble in the water, creating a ripple effect. Each action we take creates many effects in our world involving people, places, and things, sometimes with us not even being aware. I like to use the stepping-stones rather than a ladder to describe our soul progression because each action creates karma, which can move us in many different directions, propelling us quickly forward on our path, or slowing us down and away from our purpose.

What causes the triggers? Triggers are caused by our karma, people, and planetary and numerological cycles. We planned out the majority of triggers before our birth, when we mapped out our life. Let's look at each of these triggers individually. Karma is the universal law of cause and effect in action. Karma is the way the universe helps us learn our lessons. In essence, karma is what we owe to ourselves in terms of learning. It is not good or bad, rather it is neutral. Although many people view karma as a negative, it can be quite positive. We reap what we sow, whether good or bad. For example, if we do good deeds, we will receive back good things, and evil deeds will most likely bring to us unpleasant learning events. Karma can occur within the present incarnation or may be left over from past incarnations.

A karmic trigger may be something left over from a past life that was not learned, and suddenly in our current life we experience something negative. This is often the case where bad things happen to "good" people. Karma can manifest immediately in the present life, with a reaction occurring soon after the deed. Karma can also manifest on many different levels, depending on the lesson that needs to be learned. We can experience karma on the spiritual, mental, emotional, or physical levels. An example of karma triggering us on an emotional level might be where we experience a verbally abusive relationship. Karma that triggers us on a physical level might appear as an accident that leaves us paralyzed. Karma that may trigger us on a spiritual level may be where we choose parents who are Buddhists and nurture us spiritually.

People triggers are often interweaved with karma, since people are often the triggers for our karma. It is quite difficult to learn a lesson without the involvement of others. We choose willing players before our incarnation who will help us learn what we need in order to grow. For example, if we need to learn self-respect, we may choose an abusive mate. Intimate relationships are fertile ground for learning so many lessons about ourselves!

Another way our karma may be triggered that doesn't involve people is through nature. Nature is a great teacher, helping us to learn endurance, persistence, balance, cooperation, and patience. We will explore nature in greater depth in another chapter.

Planetary and numerological triggers are so vast that they each require a chapter of their own. For now I will offer a brief explanation. At our particular time of birth, the planets are placed in a pattern that creates a personality influence upon us. This planetary configuration is known as our astrology chart. We can use the chart to explain our basic personality in the present, our gifts and talents, as well as our past influences, which will manifest as our karma. The issue of when our talents will come to fruition or when our karmic challenges will appear is affected by the movement of the planets. Everything in the universe is in motion, including the planets. Various astrological techniques can map the movement of the planets and show us when these astrological triggers will affect us. Likewise, our birthdate is a set of numbers that creates a particular personality. As the years progress, the numbers change and trigger us. Numerologists also know various techniques to determine when the numbers will trigger us and in what manner. Chapters 15 and 16 will shed more light on using these two intuitive sciences to understand our time map for this lifetime.

Too many triggers close together do not allow us enough space or time to assimilate and learn from them. So why do so many of us experience triggers close together? One reason may be that we continually make bad choices that lead to difficult karmic learning. These karmic triggers come into play in addition to the triggers that were mapped out before our birth. Now suddenly the space we created in between the triggers before our birth gets filled up with triggers from present-life karma.

Another reason might be that we did not plan properly before this incarnation and didn't give ourselves enough space between the triggers. When we are a disincarnate entity planning our next physical lifetime, we may get overly ambitious and want to plan many triggers in the hopes of making a lot of progress. We often underestimate how these triggers will affect us, and hence don't plan enough space. As we all know, things often look easier from a distance, but once we get in the muck, it turns out to be more difficult. An example of this is when someone loses a loved one and falls into a deep depression and withdraws from life. Another person might turn to drugs and alcohol when the triggers become too intense.

Other people may be the cause of too many triggers. Since people have free will, they may not act according to how we thought they would when we chose them to be in our life before our birth. Perhaps we chose parents that we believed would be loving and supportive, but they turned out be abusive. These abusive parents provided us many triggers we didn't count on when we made our life plan.

We also create too many triggers when we fail to learn our lessons. For example, we have a trigger to teach us how to be independent. If we fail to learn that during our assimilation time, we will need to repeat that lesson. Hence we create another trigger to learn that lesson in the space that was meant for assimilation. By failing to learn our lessons, we create a traffic jam of triggers. We all know when we are stuck in a traffic jam, our car doesn't move. Likewise, when our triggers jam up, we often get "stuck" and can't learn anything.

Let's explore how we respond to the triggers. There are basically three ways we can respond: we can learn and become wiser, we can ignore them, or we can respond in such a way that causes us to regress. The first response is the reason we create triggers in the first place, to evolve and grow spiritually. If we respond in this way, we find it is easy to follow and stay on the path of growth we charted out before birth. Second, some people respond by ignoring the trigger. Some of us created subtle triggers that we hoped would nudge us in the right direction without causing too much drama. However, these subtle triggers are the ones we can most likely ignore. We bury our head in the sand, hoping the trigger will go away. Temporarily we may feel we won, but this is not the case. What occurs is that the trigger will reappear in a more intense manner a second time, in the hopes of getting our attention. So now what we have created is a more challenging situation that is taking up our space that was created for assimilation. Since the trigger is more difficult to ignore, we may resort to more drastic means of avoidance by escaping through drugs or alcohol. Lastly, we may respond to the trigger in a negative way that causes us to regress by creating more karmic lessons. An example of this might be a trigger to learn self-respect by choosing an abusive partner. Rather than recognizing the need for greater self-respect, we may respond by becoming abusive to our child. We often see the cycle of abuse repeated in future generations within families.

Time is different depending on where we are. When we are in spirit form, things move more rapidly than on the Earth plane. Earth is the slowest vibration, so creation moves slowly compared to the spirit realm, where creation is instantaneous. When we have a thought, it manifests instantly. It is no wonder we become frustrated with the slowness of Earth! Imagine how much quicker we would get around without having to drag our bodies along. In the spirit realm our pure energy being is not encumbered with flesh and bones, so we are in essence lighter. There is no lag time between an idea and its manifestation. We can see the instant ramifications of our thoughts. When we are in between lives and existing in our pure state of energy, there is no conscious mind filter to slow us down. We do not need to process and assimilate through the five senses. Therefore, the assimilation period is more efficient when we are out of our body.

For the many of us who lived in Mu and Atlantis, time was measured differently then. Over the years my husband and I have done hundreds of past life readings for people, many of which took place in Mu and Atlantis. These were time periods when souls were just beginning their journey in physical bodies. The Atlantean time period spanned over the course of three cycles, each concluding with a catastrophic event. My husband acts as the conductor or guide during the past life readings that we do, and so he has the opportunity to ask questions while I am in an unconscious state. When he has asked how long the person lived in Atlantis, the answer couldn't be given because time was measured differently during that era. Therefore, suffice it to know that time was measured differently in Atlantis.

One of the things that separates a master teacher from his students is his ability to manifest quickly while in the physical. We can look at the example of the master teacher Jesus, who was able to easily turn water into wine and to heal the sick instantly. There are accounts of the spiritual avatar Babaji being able to instantly manifest verbudi, a healing powder that he would offer as gifts to others. As we progress in our creating abilities and master the art of nonresistance, we will also be able to create more rapidly and with greater ease. As the struggle lessens, the manifestation is freed up to move quickly into physical form.

Time is also experienced differently while in a body, depending on our mental state. When our mind is focused on the past or future, we are resisting the present, so time appears to move slowly. When our mind is focused on the present moment, we are not resisting, and therefore time flows quickly in a seemingly effortless movement. When we are experiencing a challenge or something that causes us pain, there is resistance, so it seems time is going by slowly. When we are doing something we enjoy, then we are not resisting, and once again time seems to go by quickly. Many of us can relate to the feeling we had when we first fell in love. The feeling of ecstasy and joy was overpowering, and when we were with our beloved, we were completely unaware of time passing.

On the contrary, when we had to spend time with a rude and annoying person, time seemed to inch along at a painstakingly slow pace.

In conclusion, time is our friend, allowing us the space to assimilate, learn, and grow. We mapped out our growth plan before birth, implementing triggers throughout our life to stimulate us to gain wisdom. The way we respond to those triggers determines how quickly we grow. Life moves smoothly when we learn from the triggers, but when we ignore or respond inappropriately to a trigger, we create karmic challenges, which causes us to stagnate. Since time is nonphysical, we can notice how it appears to pass quickly or slowly, depending on our state of mind. Since many of us want to evolve and move beyond the cycle of physical birth and death, we often rush. In the next chapter we will explore the problems caused by rushing. I invite you to slow down and read the next chapter.

Activities

1. How have your ideas about time changed since reading this material?

2. Write down if you have noticed a cyclical pattern of when triggers occur in your life. What is the average time between triggers?

3. Write some significant lessons you've learned and how they have made you wiser. Celebrate your soul growth, just as you would a birthday.

4. Take notice during the day if your attention seems to be in the past or future as opposed to the present. Each time you notice your attention wandering, gently guide it back to the present. You may want to create some type of anchor that brings your attention to the present, such as a crystal or a physical movement.

5. Write down the three most recent triggers. Give details about the nature of the triggers, how you responded, and what you learned from them.

6. Notice if you are creating too many triggers in your life that are taking away your assimilation time. Examine what you are doing to create the triggers, and plan on how you can change this pattern.

7. Do you think you intentionally created a life with many triggers to become conscious and evolve quickly? Or do you believe you created a life with as few triggers as possible to enjoy an easy incarnation?

8. Write about the times you recall time passing quickly, and record details about your state of mind. Next, write about the times you recall time passing slowly, adding details about your state of mind.

Chapter 3
The Paradox of Time

The distinction between the past, present and future
is only a stubbornly persistent illusion.
—Albert Einstein

Time exists on one level, and yet it doesn't exist on another. We live in dual realities because we are spiritual beings having a physical experience. Let's explore how time affects our dual reality and how we can navigate this paradox.

From the spiritual perspective, time doesn't exist. We are eternal beings with no beginning or end. Everything is happening simultaneously, so there is no past or future.

In our physical world, time does exist. It is a structure that helps us live our lives with some type of order. It provides the conscious mind with a logical, predictable system within which it can maneuver.

Since we have this dual nature of being a spiritual being in a physical body, we can choose if we want to work within the structure of time or without it. We slip in and out of time often unconsciously throughout our lives. However, the tools in this book can help us do this consciously.

We can choose to work within the structure of time when necessary. For appointments and work schedules, time serves a great purpose and so most of us choose to work within the time structure. If we are an hourly wage earner, we clock every hour to make sure we get paid correctly. For those who procrastinate, time is a gift because it gives us a constant reminder of what we still need to do.

However, if we want to engage in a creative project or something we truly enjoy, we may find it more suitable to not work within the structure of time. Deadlines can cause stress and kill our creativity, so it can be beneficial to allow our creative endeavors to take as long as needed. If Michelangelo had a deadline for the Sistine Chapel it may not have turned out quite as beautiful. It would have been infused with the stress and fear that often accompany a deadline. Whether it's gardening, writing, painting, or dancing, when we're doing our passion, we move into the magical space beyond time. Creativity can flow easier here because there is no structure.

If we don't consciously choose whether or not to work within the structure of time, circumstances will choose for us. For example, when we are spending time with someone we adore, we often effortlessly slip into the no time zone. The enjoyment pulls us into the present moment because we really want to be at that time and place, and in the present moment we are not aware of the passing of time. This is typically a very pleasant experience.

On the other hand, we often unconsciously slip into the structure of time when we are in a boring situation or when we are experiencing discomfort or an unpleasant feeling. For example, you may be sitting in a boring class with a subject matter that doesn't interest you, and so you drift to the past or future, imagining where you would rather be. When we RESIST the present moment, it makes time appear to move slower.

In conclusion, time matters to our physical body, but not to the soul. The conscious mind and body know they only have a certain amount of time to be on the Earth, so time matters. The soul, however, knows it is infinite and has an eternity to evolve. Our dual citizenship, so to speak, allows us to work within time frames when necessary, or go beyond the constraints of time. The beauty of going beyond time allows us to experience the fullness of our soul and have spiritual experiences while in a physical body.

Activities

1. Write an epitaph. This is an opportunity for you to think about how you want to be remembered and what you want to do with the time you are given on Earth. Include both the things you want to be known for as well as the type of person you want to be remembered as.

2. Write about the moments you unconsciously slipped into a timeless state.

3. Write about the moments you consciously used time to help you finish a project or fulfill other obligations.

Chapter 4
Beyond Linear Time

Time is an illusion.
—Albert Einstein

As spiritual beings in the physical world, we are constantly trying to integrate our spiritual essence, or soul, into the physical world through the interaction between our conscious and subconscious mind. The soul, which resides in the subconscious mind, communicates with the conscious mind through the intuition and dreams. The conscious mind is bound by physical time, while the subconscious has no boundaries and therefore can see beyond the present. There are many benefits to being able to shift our focus to the expansiveness of the subconscious mind. In this chapter we will explore the benefits and the many ways we can go beyond the conscious mind and physical time to access the subconscious mind.

One of the main benefits of transcending physical time is that it helps slow the aging process. When we access the subconscious mind, we utilize the nonphysical energies that help us rejuvenate the mind and body. The aging process slows when we are focused on the soul, which is ageless. The great spiritual masters are testimony to the fact that we can defy aging. When we sleep, or go into deep meditation, we shift our consciousness to the subconscious, allowing our body to rejuvenate.

The second benefit is that when we shift our focus to the subconscious mind, we can see beyond the present moment to the past and future. We can move freely on the astral plane as well, where we can communicate with disincarnate entities.

Another benefit of transcending time is that it keeps us connected to our soul, and so has the potential of helping us evolve spiritually. The more we check in with our subconscious mind, we keep the connection to our soul strong. A strong soul connection ensures an open door to our intuition and past understandings that can help us in our present life.

With all these benefits of focusing on the subconscious mind, let's figure out how to do it! The key is to slow down the brain waves which allows us to tap the subconscious mind and transcend time. Let's take a look at the science behind the brain.

Science has shown that we have five levels of brain wave activity. When we are awake and have our focus on our conscious mind, we are experiencing Beta waves. However, as we slow our brain waves in meditation, or with other relaxation techniques, we can arrive at theta or delta. In this state we go beyond the fast-paced physical world to a more peaceful, relaxing place. This allows us to connect with the Creator, listen to our inner guidance, and align ourselves with our soul.

Gamma: These waves are measured at thirty-eight to forty-two Hz and are the fastest. These waves occur when there is simultaneous processing of information occurring in the brain areas.

Beta: These waves are measured at twelve to thirty-eight Hz and represent the brain during our normal waking state. In this state we are alert, engaged, and attentive.

Alpha: Waves measuring eight to twelve Hz are when we experience thoughts flowing quietly within, and our attention is on the present, rather than worrying about the past or future. Our brain can rest in this state.

Theta: Waves measuring three to eight Hz occur during deep meditation or sleep. We produce these waves when dreaming.

Delta: Waves measuring one-half to three Hz are

the slowest brain waves. They are produced during deep meditation or when sleeping without dreaming. Healing occurs in this stage.

There are several ways to slow down the brain waves and reach new frequencies. The easiest way is through sleep. We can also do this through meditation and other relaxation techniques. Hypnosis brain wave therapies accomplish this with music and/or lights. There are specific companies that produce music to attain the desired brain wave level. Some benefits of listening to brain wave audio sounds include greater ability to concentrate, clarity of thought, increased sense of peace, better health, more energy, and greater creativity. The music affects the brain cells by causing them to resonate to the beat. Both hemispheres of the brain become synchronized, allowing you to attain an expanded sense of awareness and relaxation.

Brain wave music creates a whole-brain state known as hemispheric synchronization, which means the left and right hemispheres of the brain work together in a state of coherence. Certain brain wave technologies use both sound and light. Visual people may find the combination of sound and light is more effective for changing their brain wave states.

Breathwork

Breathwork is wonderful for slowing down the

brain waves. A powerful breathing technique I recommend is called intuitive breathing. This method, also known as rebirthing breathwork, or liberation breathing, is a powerful way to release old thought patterns and fears. This is a technique of controlled breathing over a prolonged period of time; it is designed to release stored thoughts, feelings, and emotions from the body-mind. The inhale and the exhale breath are done in a connected, circular pattern so that there is no pause between them. This circular breathing is very beneficial because people often hold their breath when experiencing fear or anxiety; hence, many people are actually oxygen starved. This cyclical breathing is done over a period of at least forty-five minutes or longer.

There are two different methods we can choose from. One method involves breathing in and out through the nostrils. This method encourages the stimulation of our third eye, or sixth chakra. This allows us to easily tap into our intuition. Another way is to breath in and out through the mouth. This method allows more oxygen to enter and is helpful if one is congested. This method is also helpful for those who tend to easily drift off and fall asleep.

The increase in oxygen causes the release of neuromuscular patterns and allows thoughts to come to the surface so they can be released. The breath is also capable of moving through energetic and mental blocks. The breathing accesses parts of our memory that have been blocked for various reasons (hurt, pain, etc.).

We may become aware of thoughts from the past, and by continuing to breathe, we create a channel for them to be released from the body. Rebirthing allows people to go beyond their conscious mind to access the subconscious mind. In this way people may receive intuitive guidance. When we open ourselves to do this work, whatever needs to come through for our healing will present itself.

The rebirthing technique is facilitated by a trained rebirther, who acts as a coach to the client. The rebirthing coach keeps the client breathing in the cyclical pattern and writes down any important information related by the client. It is important to work with a trained rebirthing coach in the beginning before attempting to do this on your own. Any form of emotional release should also be done with a trained practitioner. It is recommended to have at least ten sessions, since most of us are like an onion with many layers of trauma to unravel.

Rebirthing breathwork was pioneered by Leonard Orr and Sondra Ray. Leonard found when he engaged in this type of breathwork that he was transported back to his birth, and hence he coined the practice "rebirthing." By revisiting his traumatic birth, he was able to clear much of the trauma that he incurred. Once the birth trauma is cleared, we are free to clear more trauma, from this life or previous lives. The breath has a wisdom of its own, and therefore will take us to the areas and memories of our past that need healing.

I have had profound experiences during my breathwork sessions that have helped me heal past life trauma. I have also received many intuitive messages for myself and others while in this altered state. Since we are open to the subconscious mind in this altered state, we can travel to the past and future. The ultimate experience in rebirthing is to experience the breathless state. After breathing for about twenty minutes or more, the body becomes full of oxygen to the point where we naturally stop breathing for a few minutes. This is a state of pure ecstasy, where we can experience ourselves as a being of light, at one with the Creator and the universe. We are weightless and feel no pain. We are truly in a timeless state. I recall after coming out of a breathless period that it seemed as if I had been in that state for hours, even though only a few minutes had passed. We can remain in this breathless state for several minutes, until the body resumes breathing.

Some effects to be aware of that can occur while doing the rebirthing breathwork include tetany and falling asleep. Tetany usually affects the periphery areas of the body such as the hands and fingers. We usually experience pain coupled with a tightening of the hands and fingers. This is a symptom of stuck energy attempting to leave the body. Therefore, the remedy is to breathe through it, allowing the breath to move the stagnant energy out. Another pattern some people fall into is the tendency to drift off for periods of time or fall into a deep sleep. It is a defense mechanism to avoid facing something that is unpleasant. The remedy is to breathe through the mouth, which allows more oxygen in, and to work with a trained rebirther. This person will be able to keep you focused by either talking to you or physically nudging you. Sometimes it can be helpful to sit up when we feel ourselves drifting off.

There are other simple breathing techniques we can use to affect our brain waves and enter the subconscious mind. The simplest technique is to set the timer for three to five minutes and focus on our breathing. We can notice the rhythm of our breath, and any changes in the rhythm as we continue breathing. We can breathe only through the nostrils or the mouth, or in through the nose and out through the mouth. Another simple breathing technique is the 4-4-4 technique, where we breathe in for a count of four, hold our breath for a count of four, and release for a count of four. Diaphragmatic breathing is another popular technique where we breathe into the abdomen and allow the oxygen to fill up our lower belly like a balloon.

Then on the exhale we allow the air to completely empty out. This is powerful because many of us are shallow breathers, never allowing the breath to go deeper than our upper chest.

Alternate nostril breathing is powerful because it promotes balance and calm within as we transcend physical time. We first place our middle finger on the left nostril while we breathe out through the right nostril. Then release the finger from the left nostril, hold the right nostril as we exhale through the left nostril. Breathe in through the left nostril, while holding the finger on the right nostril. Then we put our middle finger on the left nostril while we breathe out through the right. Continue with this process for approximately two to five minutes, or longer.

Meditation is one of the most well-known techniques to slow down our brain waves and help us transcend time. We can research the different forms of meditation until we find a style that suits us the best.

When we achieve great states of pleasure, we often enter altered states of consciousness that slow our brain waves. An example is during orgasm, where we enter a state of ecstasy so powerful that we transcend time. The endorphins that are released at orgasm can be similar to the breathless state achieved during rebirthing breath work.

When we are experiencing total love for someone or something, we are no longer in physical time. Our brain waves slow down, and we often feel spacey and have difficulty remembering what time it is! We can think back to our first love, and recall times when we were with our beloved and time seemed to stand still.

We can also alter our brain waves when we experience trauma, either in the present or the past. When trauma occurs, the emotions that accompany it get stored in our bodies. Buried emotions never die; they simply get repressed and come out at a later time. As mentioned above, intentional breathing can be powerful enough to release trapped emotions from childhood or even from past lives.

Other therapies that can release stored emotions are skin rolling, acupuncture, and acupressure. Since past life memories can easily become trapped in our cellular memory and our body, any techniques that stimulate sensitive points on our body have the ability to transport us back to the time when the original trauma occurred. In this way there is potential for releasing the pain and healing it permanently. Skin rolling, acupuncture and acupressure go deep into sensitive points to access trauma from the current life or past lives. The practitioner can hold the point for as long as needed for the person to clear the memory.

Another way to change our brain wave pattern is through the process of creating. Deep creative processes allow our mind to become still and focused which slows down the brain waves. Creating also often involves the release of the kundalini energy, which impacts brain wave activity. We often can create for hours on end without experiencing fatigue or hunger. We are so focused in the present moment that our brain waves naturally slow down.

I became a reader of the Akashic Records by learning to slow my brain waves to the point of going into a hypnotic trance. In this state, I have had the opportunity to travel back in time hundreds of years to retrieve significant past lives for people. Everything we have ever done, said, or thought about is stored in Akasha, known as mind substance. Akasha is nonphysical, and therefore not bound by physical time. It holds the records of all our lifetimes. When we learn how to tap into the Akashic Records, we essentially time travel. With patience and discipline, we can learn to access our own Akashic Records or those of others.

Past life regression is another method to travel back to one of our past lives. This process involves the assistance of a trained hypnotherapist, with extensive training in past lives. A good practitioner can help us relax and move into our subconscious mind where we can access our past lives. We know we are in that lifetime when we feel the emotions of that period. During one of my regressions I returned to a lifetime as an Aborigine where my current mother was present. We had been separated and so I was feeling very sad. I was so overcome with grief that I began crying. I remember that even though the lifetime had physically occurred over a hundred years ago, it felt as if it was happening then. I was able to understand much of the dynamics between my mother and myself from that lifetime.

Dolores Cannon was the pioneer of a process that leads people to past lifetimes called QHHT, Quantum Healing Hypnosis Technique. Dolores was instrumental in helping hundreds of people to heal trauma in this lifetime that began in the past. With her advanced hypnosis techniques, people were able to travel back in time to find answers to present-day problems.

A completely different way to move beyond physical times involves ingesting mind-altering drugs. This is what I call the easy way, since it involves no conscious will on our part. The shamans would use drugs as a way to transcend time and access altered states of consciousness. The drug ayahuasca has been used in many shamanistic ceremonies to introduce students to other worlds. Once students realize the pleasure of going beyond this dimension, they can use that motivation to continue to have those experiences without the help of mind-altering drugs.

In conclusion, since we are spiritual beings having a physical experience, it is possible to transcend time. We become aware of our limitless nature with past life regressions, Akashic Record readings, and the revolutionary method developed by Dolores Cannon, QHHT. The key is to learn how to slow down our brain waves. There are a multitude of techniques that can help us do that, such as meditation and emotional release therapies such as rebirthing breath work, skin rolling, and acupuncture. Simply by doing things we enjoy and creating can bring us into that space where we aren't bound by time. For the adventurous type, the shamanistic path of using plant medicines is another profound way to slow our brain waves and time travel.

Activities

1. Try some brain wave music to slow down the conscious mind. Hemi-Sync (hemi-sync.com) and Steven Halpern (stevenhalpernmusic. com) offer some great music.

2. Find a breathworker in your area and try some sessions. See rebirthingbreathwork. com or sondraray.com to help find a trained practitioner.

3. Try acupuncture, acupressure, or skin rolling.

4. Obtain a past life reading at:
   www.intuitiveschool.com.

5. Have a QHHT session or become a QHHT practitioner. See www.qhhtofficial.com.

Chapter 5
The Inner Work

Defer no time, delays have dangerous ends.
—William Shakespeare

The foundation for everything that happens in our life is us! Therefore, if things are moving too slowly, the first place to make changes is in ourselves. It seems odd to think we would get in our own way, but we do it all the time. In this chapter we will explore why we prefer pointing the finger outside of ourselves when things don't manifest for us, and what we can do to change that.

The main reasons we blame others for the slow pace of our manifestations is because we are either unconscious or in denial of our thoughts. It's also simply easier to blame others rather than ourselves. Lastly, many of us have become accustomed to project our problems onto others.

It is possible in some cases to speed up the timing of our manifestations by focusing on the outer things. However, it can be a slow and arduous process. For example, let's suppose I want to find a job. I could spend all my time sending out resumes, knocking on doors, etc. When I don't get the results I desire in my time frame, I can immediately blame the world. I would tell myself "those people just don't recognize talent when they see it!" Or, I might blame it on the economy. "Companies aren't hiring because of the dismal economy." It may take months or years to find a job using this method.

Everything changes when we look within. Working on ourselves is by far the quickest way to speed up our manifestations. I like to call it working from the inside out.

For example, let's suppose I want to manifest a great relationship. I can go out and buy a sexy wardrobe, change my hairstyle, and sign up for an online dating service. However, if I do nothing to work on internal issues and attitudes related to relationships, I may be waiting for years to find a compatible partner.

A large part of working on ourselves includes lining up with what we desire. Our thoughts and attitudes send out a particular vibration. If that vibration is in harmony with our desire, we will get it. Our desire is already out there waiting for us, so all we need to do is align vibrationally with it.

When we are "ready," meaning in vibrational harmony with our desire, then the time is right, and we will be able to receive it. In order to do this, we need to understand the vibration of our desire. One way to do this is to close our eyes and imagine what it would be like to have our desire, using all of our senses. The more we hold that feeling, the sooner we will attract the corresponding desire into our life. If we want to be wealthy, we can imagine ourselves dressing in fancy clothes, driving a sports car, or walking into a large home. If we want a compatible partner, we can see ourselves enjoying time with someone who exudes the qualities we admire.

If we are having difficulty aligning with our desires, we need to focus on changing our thoughts and beliefs. Some spiritual practices that can help us change are meditation, journaling, prayer, quiet contemplation, and breathing techniques. It's too broad to cover all the practices and tools to cause change, so I recommend going down this rabbit hole and experimenting until you find what works best for you.

Now I want to share some examples of people who aligned with their desires by making inner changes.

Pam Grout, author of *E Squared* and *E Cubed*, was not always a well-known author. She wrote a book titled

God Never Has a Bad Hair Day, yet it never gained much attention in the literary world. She put it on her bookshelf where it sat for many years.

Several years later she felt inspired to take it off the shelf, dust it off, and submit it to Hay House Publishing. They agreed to publish her book with minimal changes, and a new title. *E Squared* became an international bestseller. Since the content was pretty much the same as the first version, she realized that it was the internal changes she made that paved the way for the book's success.

I had a similar experience with the first book I wrote, *Soul Choices: Six Paths to Find Your Life Purpose.* I sent query letters to over one hundred publishers and got rejected by all of them. Four years passed, and on a tip from a friend, I submitted my book to Ozark Mountain Publishing. They published my book and my writing career took off. Like Pam Grout, I believe the internal changes I made allowed my book to finally gain greater exposure.

A friend of mine was devastated after her 2nd marriage ended up in a worse divorce than her first. She was determined to learn her lessons about love before jumping into another relationship. She read books, attended workshops, and did counseling for a year. She changed behaviors that were attracting the wrong types of men, and then set out to find a compatible partner. She now has a stronger connection with her inner self, and a great guy to boot!

In conclusion, if we work on ourselves, we can get more of what we want quicker. Our outer life is a reflection of our inner life. If things are moving slowly on the outside, they are most likely moving slowly on the inside. The first place to start is with ourselves, and this may be the last place we need to look. The answers are within.

<u>Activities</u>

1. Make a list of your desires. Next to each desire, write how you will feel when you manifest them. Lastly, incorporate those feelings NOW. Act as if you already have the thing you desire. For example, if your desire is to increase your income to $6,000 a month, you would feel happy, secure, free. The more you act happy, free, and secure, the closer you align to the desire and, bam, it happens!

2. Write down the things you have wanted and asked for that haven't arrived yet. Next, write who and what you have blamed for not having those things. Lastly, let go of the blame and do the activity in #1.

3. Let's get deep into our subconscious and examine any thoughts that may be blocking our desires. For example, I may desire to have a new car, yet I have thoughts that I am not worthy, or that I may never be able to afford one. Once we have determined the blockage thoughts, we can use positive affirmations or other tools to change those thoughts.

Chapter 6
Our Intuitive Clock

*I believe in intuitions and inspirations . . . I
sometimes FEEL that I am right. I do not KNOW
that I am.*
— Albert Einstein

Intuition is the key to knowing what to do and when to do
it. Intuition is the guidance that comes from our higher self,
or subconscious mind, and therefore it always acts in our
best interest and will never steer us wrong. Intuition helps
us move beyond time and manifest more quickly. In this
chapter we will learn how to recognize our intuition. We
will also look at how our intuition can help us understand
and work with time.

The first thing to know about our intuition is that
it often comes in quick flashes of insight. In order to

understand those messages, we have to quiet and slow our mind. The calmer and quieter our mind, the more we will be able to grasp these flashes of insight.

Second, our intuition gives us the whole picture, rather than all the details. It's the job of the conscious mind to flesh out any details necessary to implement the intuitive guidance.

Third, our intuition often presents us with what appears to be illogical guidance. It can take a lot of effort to override the conscious mind judgment about the message. When we do, the gifts are great.

Several years ago I received an intuitive message that our family should move to the Kansas City area. It seemed illogical since we knew only a few people in that area and didn't have any jobs lined up there. However, we trusted in the intuition, and my husband and I found ourselves in a suburb of Kansas City five months later. Overall, it turned out to be a good move for us with many opportunities.

Our intuition doesn't always tell us when to take action, so we need to take into consideration the type of guidance we receive. If the message is to turn right at the next corner, then we need to act immediately. However, if the guidance is that we should move across the country, then the time frame will be quite different. Our rate of response is also related to our level of confidence in working with our intuition. For those of us who are super confident about our intuition, we tend to take action right away. The longer we wait, our tendency to act on our intuition decreases, so I recommend acting swiftly.

With practice, I believe we can learn to tap into our intuition at will. If we discipline ourselves to connect with our subconscious mind, or inner self daily, we build rapport and trust. When we are in a quiet space, we can grasp the messages and perhaps even write them down. By meditating before bed, we can avoid a flood of insights keeping us awake. If we don't carve out quiet time to listen, then the intuition will often speak to us at inconvenient times when it may be hard to listen and respond.

Listening to our intuition can save us a lot of time. The job of our intuition is to keep us on track with our life purpose. Therefore, if we listen and follow it, we will be led on the most direct path to fulfilling our mission. When we don't listen to our intuition, we often deviate from our path.

For example, suppose our life mission involves being a nurse. If we ignore this insight, when we go to college we may choose classes that align with a different career path. When we finally heed the message, we find we are behind several years' worth of classes. A less severe example might be that while driving to work our intuition may tell us to avoid the freeway and take the side roads. We don't follow that guidance, and get stuck in a horrible traffic jam.

Our intuition will also save us time by helping us move through lessons with ease. Our intuition will always guide us to people and things that are in our best interest. Relying on our intuition can be the difference between spending years to get through a lesson versus a few months.

When we are triggered, our intuition will be there to help us through the crisis. Sometimes our intuition will even forewarn us that a trigger is on the horizon. We may even receive messages about the nature of the trigger, so we can prepare ourselves.

In conclusion, our intuition is our best friend. We can build a strong rapport and trust with our intuition by listening and then acting on the messages. Heeding our intuitive messages can save us time and effort on our journey to fulfilling our life purpose.

Activities

1. On a scale of one to ten (ten being the most), rate how confident you feel about working with your intuition.

2. Notice how your intuition communicates. Then write all the ways your intuition has communicated to you in the past.

3. Notice when your intuition communicates to you. Write down what times of the day and during what activities your intuition usually speaks.

4. If you find you need to adjust the manner in which you connect with your intuition, write what this would look like. Commit to this form of connection on a daily basis.

5. Write down any instances when your intuition steered you away from an unproductive situation or person.

6. Write about the instances when your intuition nudged you in a direction that resulted in something positive in your life.

7. Write about the instances when your intuition helped you move through a crisis.

8. Write about the times when your intuition helped you with the timing of your actions. Include as many details as possible.

Chapter 7
The Power of Visualization

We are shaped by our thoughts; we become what we think.

—Gautama Buddha

Similar to intuition, visualization is a practice that can be a great tool to help us work with time. I liken it to letting your mind do the work. Visualization is powerful because it gives our mind something to do while waiting for our "stuff" to manifest. In this chapter we will explore how to use this tool to speed up time and manifest our "stuff."

Some folks don't use this tool, claiming they don't have time. However, the more time you spend visualizing, the more time you will save down the road. When we make visualization a part of any manifestation process, we are setting ourselves up for success.

The act of using our mind to create something in our life that we desire is called *visualization*. The process involves showing our mind what we want it to create. The more accurate our image of what we desire, the more quickly our mind will manifest it. Our mind is like a camera; the better we focus in on our desire, the clearer our final product will be.

The language of the mind is images, not words. This is why visualization is so powerful, because it speaks the language our mind understands. Therefore, it is beneficial not only to write what you want, but also to draw a picture of it, or find a picture from a magazine or other source. This has turned into the popular "vision board" where people post images of all their desires for the upcoming year.

Visualization works best when we use all of our five senses. This involves closing our eyes and imagining what our desire sounds like, tastes like, feels like, looks like, and even what it smells like.

Another way to view visualization is like a mental rehearsal. After we show our mind each step, the physical activity is more likely to go smoothly and quickly. Many athletes use visualization to perfect their sport.

To begin practicing visualization, I recommend choosing an activity you want to accomplish during the day, and then spend a few minutes visualizing yourself doing the activity. Use all five senses and imagine the desired outcome. If you choose an activity you have done in the past, you can compare how much easier and quicker you were able to do it with the help of visualization.

In conclusion, using the mind energy helps us transcend physical time. Visualization makes our life a lot easier by first taking action in the mind. This mental rehearsal prepares our body, so when it's time to take physical action, our body already knows what to do!

<u>Activities</u>

1. To begin the visualization practice, choose one activity to visualize.

2. As you become more proficient, visualize your entire day.

3. You can choose your top five to eight desires and form mental images of each one. Close your eyes and see with your mind each desire, using all five senses.

Chapter 8
Relationship Timing

There is no possession more valuable than a good
and faithful friend.

—Socrates

On par with the desire to obtain "stuff" is the desire for great relationships. Most people get frustrated at how long it takes to find that special someone to spend their life with. In this chapter we'll explore how to speed up the process of finding a compatible partner by working from the inside out.

The first step many people take when they want to manifest a relationship is to make a list of all the qualities they want in another. They imagine how they want to be treated and what physical attributes they desire in the other person. It can take a long time to fill that list. So, here is another option.

First, we can start with ourselves and make a list of what we want to offer another person. We can review our qualities and talents and think how to share them in a relationship. For example, my sister is super creative, so she always helps her friends decorate their homes and shop for clothes. I do astrology readings for family and friends when they are in a crisis situation. There is always someone who needs what you have to give.

Next, we can make a list of what we want in another person. By having both lists, we have a greater opportunity of attracting the person who fits our desires, and vice versa. Once again, when we focus on both giving and receiving, we have a better chance of finding a perfect match.

We live in a vibrational universe so when we focus on what we have to offer, and what we want from others, suddenly there is an easier way for that special person to find us. When each person puts out their vibrational message to the universe, everything gets rolling!

We can do this same process to find our dream job quickly. We start by making a list of what we have to offer and how we can enhance the company. Next, we make a list of what we want to receive from the job in terms of salary and benefits. This creates a giving and receiving and it not only speeds things up, it also increases the chances that we will get a job perfectly suited for us. It's more of a win-win for both employer and employee.

In conclusion, it's important we know ourselves and what we have to offer others, as well as what we want to receive. Relationships are a perfect place to practice giving and receiving. The clearer we are on what we want to share with others, the better chance we have of finding satisfying relationships.

Activities

1. Make a list of what you want to offer another person. As a starting point, look at your gifts and skills.

2. Make a list of what you want in another person.

3. If you are looking for a job, or currently employed somewhere, make a list of what talents and skills you want to offer.

Chapter 9

Universal Laws Change the Game

Time is the most valuable thing a man can spend.
—Theophrastus

There are thirteen universal laws that affect everyone on the planet. These laws work whether we are aware of them or not. They are energetic laws, and therefore they can affect time and our rate of growth. The laws create a framework for evolution to exist. In this chapter we will explore six of the laws that most directly relate to time. I will describe how to wield these laws so we can gain more control over time.

The universal laws are not meant to slow us down, but rather are designed to help us speed up our evolution. By understanding the laws, we can use them to our advantage and become the master of time. If we misuse the laws, we can slow down our growth. Likewise, if we go against a physical law, we may lose years of our life in prison.

The laws are interrelated, so that when we activate one law, we put into motion other laws. Conscious use of the laws generates energy, which will create a ripple effect in our life, propelling us forward on our journey.

If we violate a physical law, we know there will be an effect at some point, but we don't always know when. Likewise, we don't always know when we will experience the effects of a universal law. Much of the timing depends on the intention and clarity of our mind at the time we enacted the law.

Let's take a deep dive into six universal laws that affect time in powerful ways.

The Universal Law of Existence

This law brings attention to learning about our identity. Our core identity is who we are apart from all of the things we identify with being, such as a man, woman, teacher, or actress. We enact this law when we identify as a spiritual being. We are infinite, powerful beings, and this realization alone helps us transcend the confines of time traps.

As energy beings, we have no beginning or end, and so in essence, we have all the time in the world. This is a game changer for those who pressure themselves into thinking they only have one lifetime to get everything done. Similarly, we can tap our true power base and create so much more with the time we have on Earth when we embrace our spiritual identity.

EXERCISE: To enact this law I recommend practicing some form of meditation daily.

The Universal Law of Attraction

This is one of the most familiar laws to most people because it affects our lives profoundly. There is a great desire to understand this law because most of us are always wanting something, whether it be a new car or a romantic relationship.

We begin activating this law by imagining something we desire, similar to visualization. This thought radiates out from our mind like a magnet, attracting people, places, and things to help us fulfill our desire.

The big question then becomes, when will I get my stuff? The first mistake people make is giving up too soon. When our desire doesn't appear within our time frame, doubt and despair often set in. If we succumb to the despair, we may abandon our desire. TIMING is the biggest reason many of us abandon our desires.

The good news is we CAN AFFECT THE TIMING of when we get our stuff! If we consciously put this law into action in our lives, we can speed up the manifestation process.

EXERCISE: Make a list of your top five to ten desires.

Here are some **TIPS** to follow:

1. State your desire as if you already have it. Example: I am a published author.

2. State your desire in the positive. Example: I have a zero balance on all my credit cards. The mind doesn't distinguish between negative and positive, only on what you are focusing on. If I say, "I don't have debt," the message to my mind is DEBT.

3. Make your desire quantifiable. You want to be able to identify when you have manifested your desire, so avoid ambiguity. Instead of saying, "I have more peace in my life," think about what your life would look

like when you have peace and put that in your statement. For example, "My home is a quiet, cozy refuge where I can relax."

4. Write down your desires on a paper where you can easily see them and access them. The more you focus on the desires, the quicker they will manifest.

5. Avoid DOUBT and NEGATIVITY. If you believe you can't have what you want, that thought can cancel out your desire. The doubts often creep up from your subconscious mind and infiltrate your desires like little invaders. You can wipe them out by redirecting your attention to what you do want.

6. My favorite tool is to think of someone that has done something INCREDIBLE. I write out what the person did in the following manner: 'If _____ (person's name) can do _____ (person's amazing feat) then I can surely _____ (your desire.)

Example: If <u>BEETHOVEN</u> could <u>COMPOSE 722 WORKS</u>, I can surely <u>WRITE ONE SCREENPLAY.</u>

The Universal Law of Proper Perspective

If we use proper perspective, we may be able to speed up the manifestation of our desires. The key is to use discernment to know what would be best for us to manifest. Discernment helps us align with our soul needs for growth.

Imagine we are fourteen years old and are focusing on attracting a new Ferrari. Since we wouldn't even have a driver's license at that time, it would not be something we could use at that point in our life. Since it is out of alignment with our needs, we would probably have difficulty manifesting it. And if we do manifest something that we failed to use proper perspective with, it may bring us more problems than benefits.

EXERCISE

1. Make a list of things you manifested without using proper perspective. Reflect on the problems these things caused and the level of difficulty it took to manifest them.

2. Review the list of desires you wrote in the law of attraction exercise and put them in order from most to least important.

The Law of Prosperity and Abundance

If we want more money, we need to understand the laws of prosperity and abundance. In order to fully use these laws, we need to expand our ideas beyond physical wealth. To invoke the law of prosperity, we simply need to use what we know. Sounds simple enough, but several things can get in the way. If we lack confidence or don't trust what we know, we probably won't share it. If we know something and fail to respond, we lose prosperity. Sharing sets everything in motion.

The law of abundance states that as we aid others to abundance, we will be abundant in return. This law is about GIVING. Life is a game of you go FIRST. When we wait around for someone else to give to us, we may be waiting a long time. This slows things down! If we want our STUFF sooner, the best way to make that happen is to GIVE. The best way to give is to not simply give a man a fish, but rather to teach him how to fish. In this way we will feed him for a lifetime. Imagine if we went a step further and taught that man how to teach others to fish. This would speed up events for ourselves, as well as for the man we taught and all the people he would go on to teach.

The phrase "Use it or lose it" encapsulates this law. Imagine buying a bunch of food and never eating it. The food would rot and become useless. All the energy it took to grow and harvest the food would have been in vain. Likewise, when we learn something but don't use it or pass it along to someone else, it is useless. We also risk forgetting what we learned!

If we want to SPEED UP our learning, the best way is to teach others what we know. Imagine how slow things would go in our lives if people never took the time to teach us anything. We can transcend time and grow leaps and bounds when we have a good teacher.

In conclusion, whether we want more money, a bigger house, or more friends, we can speed up our abundance by SHARING OUR KNOWLEDGE and TALENTS and TEACHING others.

EXERCISE

1. Make a list of all your skills. Formulate a plan for teaching these skills to others.

2. Make a list of the best teachers you had. Reflect on all the things you learned from them.

The Law of Relativity

This law states that one thing leads to another. We can observe that as we set one thing into motion, it leads to another event, and so on. It also states that all things are connected and therefore what happens to one part of the whole affects the remainder of the whole.

When we throw a stone into a pond it sets out a series of ripples affecting the rest of the pond. Every choice we make sets off a series of events that all lead to something else. Think of all the events that are set into motion when two people get married.

When we want to manifest something by a certain date, the law of relativity helps speed up time by setting into motion a series of events that will lead us to our desire.

EXERCISE:

1. Write one action that you took and draw lines emanating outward showing all the things that occurred as a result.

2. Reflect on a postive, helpful action you recently took, and the effect it produced.

3. Reflect on a negative, unproductive action you recently took, and the effect it produced.

The Law of Cause and Effect

For every action there is a reaction. What goes up must come down. Karma is a function of this law and helps ensure we will experience and learn our lessons. When we talk about vertical time versus horizontal time, the key to moving to vertical is understanding karma. As we grow in awareness, we travel vertically and gain wisdom.

Karma is not a punishment, rather it is a gift because it brings us balance. When we learn quickly, we don't get stuck in the webs of karma, which can slow us down. For example, when we don't learn our lessons, we create a debit in our spiritual bank account. Now we must credit our account to bring it back to balance by learning some sort of lesson. That is our karma. If we learn the lesson the first time, we advance in the game of life. If we don't learn the lesson, we have to keep going back to the same spot on the game board until we learn it. This sets us back and we lose time.

For example, a woman who is married to an abusive man doesn't learn the lesson of building self-worth, so she stays with him for twenty years. When she finally gains self-respect and value, she leaves him. We may hear that woman comment, "I just wasted twenty years of my life with that jerk!"

In conclusion, we have a set of universal laws that we can use to gain more control over time in our life. Simply by enacting the law of existence, we break free from the structure of time, because we know we are timeless, limitless beings. The law of attraction engages our powers of visualization so we can manifest quickly. The law of proper perspective helps us use our power of discrimination to focus on what is most important and to move away from other distractions that can slow us down. The law of relativity reminds us that once we activate one law, it creates a ripple effect that leads to something else. The law of prosperity and abundance teaches us that staying in the flow and giving and receiving helps to move any suffocating time barriers. The law of cause and effect is a great teacher, helping us learn our lessons quickly so we don't waste time repeating the same lesson over and over again!

Enjoy the activities embedded in this chapter after each corresponding universal law.

Chapter 10
Service Gives Us More Time

The best way to find yourself is to lose yourself in the service of others.

—Mahatma Gandhi

One of the easiest, most pleasurable and rewarding ways to speed up manifestation is to be of service to others. Being of service puts the ball in our court. When we are waiting to receive something, we are really at the whim of the universe to give us what we want. However, when we give, we set everything in motion. We become the driver of the car, rather than the passenger. Let's take a journey into the benefits of service.

When we serve others, our attention shifts from us to them. This shift can help free up blockages within ourselves, allowing us to move forward. When we become fixated on our own problems, this can really slow us down! We tend to focus on the problem rather than the solution. However, by putting our attention on serving another, our vision expands and we may find the solution to our problem. In essence, we get out of our own way, allowing the door to open for things to happen.

We don't focus as much on our worries and doubts about whether we can manifest something when we are serving others. This often frees up the blockages, allowing the universe to deliver our desires.

When I was starting up my astrology business, it was taking longer than I anticipated to build up my clientele. One day a family member was having a challenge, so I offered her a free reading. A few weeks later she referred one of her friends to me, and my clientele expanded. I have heard many other stories from self-employed folks who grew their business by openly giving.

We all have a spiritual bank account. Each time we are of service, we make a deposit. Then when we want to receive something from the universe, our spiritual bank account is there with plenty of credits. This is similar to a physical bank. If we have money in the bank and we see the perfect car we've been dreaming of, we have the cash to buy the car immediately.

Likewise, when we aren't manifesting the "stuff"

we want in our time frame, it may be because our spiritual bank account is empty. For example, I had a friend who wanted to move out of her apartment into a new place. She had to keep changing the move date because she couldn't find any friends to help her. Her spiritual bank was empty! She admitted that she never stuck her neck out to help others and rarely gave first. Eventually she had to pay a moving company.

Tithing is another way to fill up our spiritual bank account. When we give money, we receive back ten times the amount we gave. I'd say that's a pretty good ROI (return on investment) and one of the greatest ways to speed up the wealth process. It will take us longer to build up our spiritual savings account if we stuff our money under a mattress and never share it.

When we offer our talents to another in service, the receiver usually wants to thank us in some way. If we deny them the ability to give to us, the circle of service is not complete. If we fail to give or receive, we block the energies. Giving and receiving puts us in the ebb and flow of the universe, and this is what service is all about.

In conclusion, serving benefits the giver as much as the receiver. Just like in tennis, the person who serves the ball sets everything in motion. If we want to speed up the manifestation process, we can reach out and see how to help another person manifest what he or she wants.

These activities will get the ball rolling and fill up our spiritual bank account.

<u>Activities</u>

1. Make a list of your gifts and talents.

2. Write about how you can use these gifts in service to others.

3. Let's get an estimate on how many credits you have in your spiritual bank account. Make a list of the ways you have served others throughout your life.

Chapter 11
Slow Is the New Fast

Do not dwell in the past, do not dream of the future,
concentrate the mind on the present moment.
—Gautama Buddha

Humans are always looking to do things faster. In our quest for efficiency and speed, we often lose our connection to who and what is around us. Technology is speeding up our lives in ways we never could have imagined. In this chapter we will explore the ego's role in our lives, and the many reasons we rush through life in the areas of food, health, money, and relationships. Next, we will learn the problems that we create by rushing and forcing things to go beyond their natural rhythm. Last, we will explore how we rush our evolutionary process of reincarnation.

Let's begin by exploring why we rush. At the core,

it's our ego that wants to rush getting things because it believes it is not complete. It lives in fear and dwells in scarcity consciousness, making us believe we better hurry and grab things first before someone else does. In those times we must remember we live in an abundant universe that is always on our side.

The ego wants us to believe that this is our only lifetime, so we better rush and get everything done before we die. The ego keeps us immersed in physical thinking and the belief that the physical is all we have. To distract us from our inner self and any connection to our spirituality, the ego keeps us perpetually busy chasing after desires, like a hamster on a wheel. This constant distraction keeps us separated from exploring our deeper spiritual roots.

The big lie of the ego is that when we finally get the stuff we want, we will be happy. Unless we are first happy within, the things we are going after will only be a temporary fix.

Now we'll dive into the four main areas in our lives where we rush, and the associated problems. We hurry in the areas of food, health, money, and relationships. As previously mentioned, the root reason is due to ego-perpetuated fears. In the area of food, the fear thought is usually scarcity. The ego makes us believe if we don't eat a lot and quickly, we will lose out. Most of us eat way too fast to properly digest our food. Rapid eating doesn't give our brain time to signal that we are full, so we keep on eating, often leading to weight gain. Our urge for quickness created the whole "fast-food" generation where quicker was favored over quality. McDonald's revolutionized the way we prepare and eat food. Fast foods have caused a multitude of problems, from weight gain to overall toxicity.

In our desire to get food to cook quickly, we invented the microwave oven. The safety of microwave ovens has been questioned by many scientists since they can alter the chemical structure of foods, decrease red and white blood cell count, and produce radiolytic compounds.

Now scientists have taken the quick-food craze to a whole new level with the invention of genetically modified foods. In an attempt to force food to grow more quickly and be more pesticide resistant, scientists have created these "franken foods" that can lead to problems such as food allergies, liver problems, reproductive complications, antibiotic resistance, and a decrease in the nutritional value of the food. We only have to look at the health of our population to see the problems rushing food has caused us.

Food eaten at the wrong time can be poison, or at the least very unappetizing. However, when eaten at the right time, food can be quite pleasurable. Several fruits can be deadly if eaten unripe, such as lychees, winter cherries, and ackees. Undercooked meats such as pork can also negatively affect us, leading to parasites and other food-borne bacteria.

In the area of health, we want sickness and pain to go away as quickly as possible. Since the ego makes us believe that we are purely physical beings, the thought of death is frightening to many of us. The fear of sickness and death has led us astray in our attempt to maintain our health. Scientists have invented pills that make pain go away almost instantly. When we don't recover quickly enough from a cold, we often resort to an antibiotic. Women want to get pregnant quickly and may resort to forcing the body into pregnancy with fertility drugs and other procedures. Likewise, women have become impatient with pregnancy to the point where they schedule a C-section before the baby is ready to come out naturally. Sometimes people even rush their own death with euthanasia.

We see the ramifications of rushing on our health where many people have become dependent on painkillers, while others are suffering the side effects of other medications. The overuse of antibiotics has led to the creation of resistant super bugs and the destruction of our gut flora. Fertility drugs have led to multiple births and an increase in birth defects. Many C-sections are unnecessary and cause complications associated with severe bleeding. The most serious karmic implications can occur when we end our life prematurely. Using euthanasia or other methods to end our life has countless ramifications since we are denying ourselves the experience that we set out to create.

So many of us have money fears because we buy into the ego's thoughts about scarcity and separateness. When we believe we are separate from the Creator, it is hard to have trust that the universe will provide for us. Therefore, we are often greedy with our money and feel compelled to get rich quick. Rather than saving our money and watching it grow over time, we engage in risky investment schemes. The results can be disastrous. Many people have lost their entire retirement with risky investment schemes.

In the area of relationships, the ego fears being alone because it convinces us that we are separate from others and our Creator. Our true self knows it is never alone because the Creator is always with us. Meanwhile, the ego pushes the false belief that if we are not with another person, we will suffer. It is this false belief that causes us to rush into relationships. We often will rush to the altar, rather than enjoying getting to know the person through a courtship. The obvious danger is divorce. Divorce is a major trigger that can teach us a lot about ourselves. However, many people don't use the assimilation period and prefer to rush back out and start dating. This often leads people to marry the same type of person over and over again. Rushing friendships can lead us to choose the wrong kinds of people to associate with.

One negative effect of rushing that affects all areas of our life is that it blocks us from our inner guidance. We need space and quiet to hear the voice of our soul. It is the guidance from our higher self that will help us learn from the experience and lead us to our next step. Our intuition is such a critical piece to our development, we will explore it in great detail in the next chapter.

We must be cautious when people rush us, because it usually means they want to control us in some way. When someone rushes us into a decision, it may be because they don't want us to reflect on the choice. If someone wants to convince us of something, he will try and get us to make a decision as fast as possible. A typical example is a car salesman who may take hostage of our mind and move us through the car-buying process so fast that we don't have time to hear our inner guidance. Salesmen know that when our inner guidance and reasoning kick in, we are more apt to say no to their offers.

Another attitude which causes us to rush is desperation. The ego is usually behind our feelings of desperation, which causes us to rush decisions that usually turn out to be unproductive choices. I can recall several times in my life when I acted out of desperation and paid the price for months or years afterward. One particular incident involved a rental property my husband and I had. A month had gone by and we still had not found any renters, so we were both feeling a bit desperate. We finally received an application from a couple that we both had the feeling might be trouble, but we blocked those intuitive thoughts because we were so anxious to rent the property. Needless to say, the pair turned out to be disastrous. When we are tempted to act out of desperation, we must remind ourselves that waiting a bit may earn us time in the end.

The bigger question involves whether or not we can rush our incarnations. My husband and I have done hundreds of past life readings for people over the years that have confirmed the tendency for people to rush back too quickly into another lifetime without adequate preparation. Many rushed back because they believed they could learn quicker in a body than in the spiritual realms. The purpose of spending time on the astral plane before incarnating again is to assimilate our past life and learn as much as possible from our experiences. The time between lives is also meant for us to prepare for our next lifetime. While on the astral plane we have loving spirit guides who work with us to learn and evolve. If we rush back too quickly to Earth, we may miss out on many of their teachings.

Meanwhile, it is imperative that we develop

patience. For kids, and even adults, I recommend the book *The Tortoise and the Hare*. It reveals the timeless message that the slow and steady ultimately prevail in the end. Many spiritual practices are designed to bring us peace and patience. Meditation is my first recommendation to slow down and receive the guidance necessary to achieve our goals without rushing. Breathing techniques, such as intuitive breathing, are also beneficial. I like the affirmation "It's all about cycles." This helps me, whether things I like are happening or things I don't like are occurring. Knowing that everything will eventually pass helps us get through the tough times and gives us hope for happier events in the future.

In conclusion, we often believe that rushing will further us along our path, but the irony is that it ultimately usually slows us down. Our motivation to rush stems from misleading fears of our ego. The fear-based ego believes in lack and separateness, two attitudes that encourage us to move quickly through life. The ego-driven mind rushes in four significant areas; food, health, money, and relationships. This causes us countless problems, from bad health to financial problems and divorce. Not only do we rush while in a body, but many of us also rush our time in between lives. In our quest to get back in a body, we may lose out on valuable assimilation time. Many of us would find it helpful to know when to take action and when to slow down. I believe if we listen to our intuition, we will receive this valuable insight. The next chapter shows us how nature can help us slow down and get in a rhythm that is in tune with our being.

Activities

1. Write down the reasons you feel compelled to rush.

2. Identify any false egoic beliefs that cause you to rush and replace them with affirmations based on the truth about your timeless existence and relationship to the Creator.

3. Identify how you rush in the areas of food, health, finances, and relationships.

4. Write concrete ways you can change the way you approach food, health, finances, and relationships.

5. Reflect and journal about a time in your life when you acted out of desperation. What did you learn from this situation?

6. Make a list of choices that would have turned out better if you had not acted so hastily.

7. Look back at those things you got in life and assess honestly if you had gotten them sooner, would you really have been ready?

Chapter 12
Nature Is Our Timekeeper

*To every thing **there** is a **season**, and **a time** to*
every purpose under the heaven: A time to be born,
*and **a time** to die; **a time** to plant, and **a time** to*
pluck up that which is planted; . . . A time to weep,
*and **a time** to laugh; **a time** to mourn, and **a time** to*
dance.

—Ecclesiastes

Nature doesn't rush, and her timing can be seen through the cycles and elements. Being in nature can help us adjust our time clock and get more in the flow. The four elements—fire, earth, air, and water—each teach us something about time cycles. The elements move at their own rate, so we can learn to use the elements to affect time in our lives. In this chapter we will explore the four seasons and four elements and learn how we can use them to transform our lives.

The energies of each season are quite different and the key to flowing with time is to harmonize with them. We can learn how to do this by exploring each of the four seasons.

Summer: Most people agree summer goes by way too fast! We could attribute this to several things. It is typically a time when we take vacations, and since we are having fun, the time seems to go by fast. The weather is typically pleasant, so we have all our attention focused in the present. This season is about enjoyment of the present moment, when so many cherished fmaily memories are made on vacations. It is a time of action when we engage in fun outdoor activities.

Fall: This season is all about adapting to change and preparing. We have to learn to shift. We are in between the speed of summer and the slowness of winter. Imagine driving a car—this is the shifting of gears from fast to slow. How well we can shift is the challenge of fall. When we have difficulty our body may fall ill as it tries to adjust to the changing temperatures and activities. We can benefit with extra meditation time and body care. Nature reminds us that fall is a time to prepare for the long winter, as we see squirrels burying their nuts and bears enjoying their last feasts before a long hibernation with no food.

Winter: This season teaches us to slow down. It is a time to rest and take stock of our lives. The water that flowed in the spring, summer, and fall now turns to ice. The cold and often inclement weather invites us to stay inside and engage in quiet activities. Although our physical activities slow down, that doesn't mean our mental activities need to slow down. As a writer, I enjoy the permission mother nature gives me to enjoy a cup of hot cocoa and write all day without guilt. I have no garden screaming at me to pull the weeds, or a child home from school wanting to go to the pool. I can meditate without the loud lawn mowers in the distance.

Spring: The word itself implies action—to spring forward. After the slowness of winter months, everything in nature begins to speed up. It is a transitional month like fall, where we are moving from slow to fast. Again, extra time for meditation and care of the body are important during this transitional phase. It is a time where we plant seeds and watch them grow, so likewise it is a period for taking action on the ideas we planted over the winter. The weather gets nicer, so we have more desire to be outside and be active. The challenge in spring is to not wish it away because we want summer so badly. It is one of the best seasons to understand cycles since we see how the death of winter transitions into new life.

The Four Elements

> *One touch of nature makes the whole world kin.*
> —William Shakespeare

Fire

Fire moves quickly and abruptly. It doesn't take much to get the fire moving, and once it starts it is difficult to stop it. Its' energetic, impulsive nature gives it the ability to transform. Within minutes wood is turned to ash. When a forest burns down, the ground is renewed and growth can begin again.

Fire Therapy

There are many ways we can use fire as a therapeutic agent in healing and transformation. Fire therapy can help when we are stagnant. We can sit in front of a fire and allow the fire to burn away old, unwanted, or negative thoughts that are causing the stagnation. We can also use fire to help us build concentration. We can sit and gaze into a fire or a candle for ten minutes or more. As we do this, we can relax the mind and slow the brain waves down. I have had the experience of being in front of a fire for hours, yet it seemed like only thirty minutes had gone by. We can use fire to help us move beyond a difficult trigger by helping us process and learn difficult lessons quickly. Fire is essential in healing mental, emotional, and physical ailments.

Air

Air shares many of the qualities of fire and also stimulates it. The quality of air is related to the movement of thought and moves quickly like fire. When our thoughts are uncontrolled, they are like the wind, blowing in every direction.

Air Therapy

Air therapy can be used when we have become stagnant or need to speed things up. Breathwork is the main therapy related to air. Please refer to the many forms of breathwork described in Chapter 4.

Water

Water typically moves slower than fire and air. Water brings us back into balance by helping us get into the flow—and back to our natural rhythm. If you feel things are moving too fast or too slow in your life, water therapies are recommended. Water nourishes our ideas and helps things grow. It is a balance and support system that can speed up healing and help move us through a challenge.

Water Therapy

Water therapy is particularly beneficial in calming our emotions. If someone had a challenging emotional event, they can become stuck in time at that age. For example, a person can be thirty years old, yet emotionally be stuck at age fourteen due to some emotional event. Water therapies include swimming, watsu, underwater breath work with a snorkel, and meditating in water.

Earth

Earth moves more slowly than any of the other elements. Earth brings us into the present moment. Earth is more cautious than air or fire. When we are in doubt about taking action, Earth energy helps us be content with where we are at. Earth reminds us that sometimes no movement is better than movement.

Earth Therapy

If we are focused on the future or the past, I recommend earth therapies to bring us into the NOW. Some common earth therapies include massage, reflexology, walking, gardening, cooking and preparing healthy food.

Combining elements can be powerful. For example, we can do breath work in water, combining air and water. Or we can sit in a bath surrounded by candles, combining fire and water.

In conclusion, the seasons have an impact on the timing of our lives. The more we get in sync with the seasons, the better we will know when to take action and when to sit back. If we find ourselves in a particular funk, we can use a therapy related to the four elements. Fire and air move us out of stagnancy and give us the zest to move quickly. Water helps us when our emotions are erratic or stuck, usually related to a traumatic event from the past. Earth therapies bring us to the present moment in time.

<u>Activities</u>

1. First, determine your relationship with time. Do you feel things are moving too slow or fast? Do you feel you are stagnant and emotionally stuck?

2. Based on your answer in number 1, choose an elemental therapy to help you get in sync with time.

Chapter 13
Prepare the Foundation

*By failing to **prepare**, you are **preparing** to fail.*
—Benjamin Franklin

When something doesn't happen in our desired time frame, one reason may be that we haven't done the necessary preparation. Lack of preparation is one of the main reasons it can take a long time to manifest things. In this chapter we will explore how preparation is a game changer, and why we may be tempted to skip this important step. We will also uncover why the cure to speeding things up is to prepare ourselves.

One reason we may fail to prepare is because we are impatient or lazy. Many of us want to go from step A to Z, without having to do the work. Another reason may be that we simply don't know what to do to prepare. Lastly, we may think we don't have time, and that things will just work out once we get our "stuff." Whatever the reason, skipping this step is a recipe for disaster, sometimes completing stopping the manifestation of our desire.

The most important part of any preparation plan should include visualization. It doesn't matter if we want to prepare for a dinner party or a new job, we always benefit and speed things up by first showing our mind what we want. Our mindset is another key part of the preparation process. Confidence in our ability to have what we want is key. An easy way to gain this confidence is by being prepared. A sense of worthiness will also help us effortlessly receive our desires.

When we have this positive mindset, next we can "get out of our own way." This involves removing any limitations in our thinking that can interfere with our desire.

Negative thoughts such as "I can't" or "It won't happen" need to be erased and replaced with positive affirmations.

After we have prepared ourselves and our mind, then we need to take the physical action. The steps will be different depending on the goal. I recommend consulting with a specialist related to your goal to help you properly prepare.

Let's look at some examples of preparations we can make.

1. If we want to sell our house, we can spend money marketing it, but if the house isn't fixed up, we've wasted our money. First impressions are important, and so our property can lose potential buyers by showing it before it is ready. I once flipped a mobile home and was discouraged because it wasn't selling. We spent most of our efforts fixing up the interior, but the curb appeal wasn't good. Finally when we painted the outside and worked on the garden, the home sold within a week. A competent realtor will help you get your house in tip-top shape for a quick sale.

2. When we want to have a baby, we need to do a lot of preparation. First, we prepare our relationship. If we aren't married, we begin looking for a mate, and if we already have someone we do what's necessary to be able to bring a baby into the space. If our relationship is not strong enough, the stress of a baby can destroy it. We need to prepare financially to be able to take care of a child. Next, we have to do the physical preparation of getting our body healthy. If we fail to prepare our body, we risk having a miscarriage or unhealthy child. Then we need to prepare our house, the "nesting" phase that most women go through, which includes

setting up the nursery and baby proofing the rest of the home.

3. If we want to publish a book, we need to research, write, and then do a thorough job editing it and getting critiques from others. I recall the first screenplay I wrote. I was so excited to send it off to agents, I skipped many steps, which is why I didn't get any bites.

4. We can't skip the important example of relationships. I've been there, like many of you, praying for my marriage partner to come into my life. I thought graduating from college meant I was ready for marriage. Today I look back at my twenty-year-old self and laugh. I was totally not prepared for my life partner back then. Little did I know how much preparation work I had in front of me! If you're struggling in this department, I recommend the book *Soul Choices: Six Paths to Fulfilling Relationships*. Preparation for a lifelong relationship begins with ourselves by doing the self-development work to discover who we are. Then life becomes our relationship teacher, giving us challenges so we can mature. The more prepared we are, the quicker we can manifest an ideal partner.

In conclusion, when we don't prepare, we often spin our wheels trying to make something happen, rather than just doing the necessary preparation work. Everything requires a different preparation protocol. When in doubt about whether we're prepared to receive our desire, keep preparing! The irony is the more time we spend in preparation, the more time we will actually save ourselves in the long run. If something is not happening, it may be the universe's way of saying, "there is more preparation to be done."

<u>Activities</u>

1. Make a list of your top five to eight desires.

2. Next to each desire, write the steps necessary to prepare to receive the desire.

Chapter 14
Events out of Sequence

Time and space are modes by which we think and
not conditions in which we live.
—Albert Einstein

Have you ever had an unexpected event that at first seemed
like a terrible thing, until other events that rolled out later
proved the event was actually a blessing? This is what I
like to call an event out of sequence. In this chapter we
will explore this phenomenon and how it can change our
perception of the sequence of events.

Our conscious mind prefers the logical and the
known. It needs the security of knowing that the events
of our life will follow in the order that we want. Yet as
most of us have experienced at least once in our lives,
this is not always the case. When an event happens out of
the sequence the conscious mind was expecting, all chaos

can break loose in our minds. How many times have we said to ourselves "this wasn't supposed to happen yet!" or "why isn't this happening already?"

The conscious mind dislikes uncertainty. The problem is usually not the waiting, but rather the ambiguity of whether or not what you want will arrive. Or in the case of an event happening too soon or unplanned, the ambiguity revolves around if you will be able to deal with this. The ego, which can greatly influence our conscious mind, likes to be in control and doesn't welcome things out of sequence.

Living in a state of ambiguity that time often places us in requires trust and faith. The more that we can cultivate these qualities, the more time will become our friend. It can give us peace of mind by trusting that there is a reason events unfold the way they do.

Suppose our conscious mind maps out a sequence of events that it hopes will lead to a particular conclusion. We may plan on going to college, graduating with a degree in math, and getting a job as a math teacher. However, let's suppose we run out of funds our second year and have to take time off to earn money. At first, we may be devastated that our plan is being delayed. However, suppose that year we work at a restaurant and discover a love of cooking. This may cause us to completely change our career direction and attend cooking school and become a chef.

In retrospect, the event out of sequence was the best thing that could have happened to us.

Often these events simply have not been given the opportunity to mature. We can practice patience and allow the event to unfold. Imagine if we plucked an unripe avocado and ate it. It would be hard as a rock and wouldn't taste very good. When we allow fruits and vegetables to ripen naturally, they become the delicious blessings from the earth they were meant to be.

Culturally we are conditioned to believe things are supposed to happen in a particular order. First we date, then get married, and then have a baby. This sequence is all too often disrupted and may lead to being negatively judged for not following the acceptable societal sequence. If we can unshackle ourselves from the sequence norms, we can free ourselves to do things in our own way at our own pace. Imagine the stigma of being called a spinster that used to follow women who weren't married by age thirty! This harsh conformity to societal sequences can leave us in despair, thinking that a particular opportunity is over for us because of our age.

The events of our lives are like stepping-stones, each one leading us to something else. We often don't know what the next step is, or where it will lead, so trusting that there is a larger plan that we can't see yet is helpful. Oftentimes there are preparation steps that we didn't plan on. We have already discussed in previous chapters the importance of preparation. Events out of sequence are often preparation steps we didn't know we needed. For example, we may feel we are ready to have a baby, but suddenly our mother becomes ill and we have to focus on being a caretaker for her for a year. Unknowingly, this event was a necessary step in preparing us to be a mother.

Here is a story from my friend Trisha, which I think beautifully illustrates the importance of trusting in the unfoldment of events out of sequence.

A Delayed Flight

Trisha was anxiously awaiting her flight back home during a layover in Chicago when she heard the dreaded announcement that the plane was delayed for two more hours. She decided to get some lunch, and as soon as she entered the restaurant she recognized an old college buddy. She discovered that he had recently started a marketing company and was looking for employees in various states throughout the country. Trisha had experience in marketing and was tired of her current job. This meeting led to Trisha gaining new employment that was more in alignment with her purpose than her previous job.

This is testimony to the idea that sometimes an

event out of sequence can be the answer to our prayers.

In conclusion, the difficulty people have of living in ambiguity causes us to detest events out of sequence, or delayed events. When this happens, our mind often goes to worry and fear, rather than peace. The solution is to surrender into the present moment, even when events aren't rolling out as planned.

Activities

1. Write about a significant event out of sequence. Include your feelings and emotions.

2. On a scale of one to ten, ten being the best, rate how well you deal with ambiguity.

3. Write about an event out of sequence that prepared you for your next step.

Chapter 15
Count Your Cycles by Numbers

Let every man be master of his time.
—Shakespeare

In our attempts to understand and work with time, we have sought out indicators from the universe to guide us. One such tool is numbers. In this chapter we will explore the power of numbers to help us understand the timing of events in the universe and our own lives.

Numerology is an intuitive science that uses numbers as a guide to understand the timing and cycles of the world. I love numerology because of its simplicity. The method used in this book is based on the Western Pythagorean system. Pythagoras was a philosopher, astronomer, and astrologer who revealed the mystery of numbers to the world. Numerologists have discovered that every number expresses a certain vibration, or personality. We are drawn to a certain number because of the qualities and characteristics it represents. No number is better than another; each is unique and necessary to embody the different energies that exist. Each number has both positive and negative aspects. It is up to us to determine how we will apply the gift of numbers—the numerical influences—in our life.

Numerology works predominantly with the numbers 1 through 9. Therefore, when we add a series of numbers, we reduce two-digit numbers to a single digit with (in most cases) the exception of the master numbers, 11 and 22. Each number expresses the opposite qualities of the preceding number. For example, 1 expresses the energy of independence, leadership, and individuality, while 2 represents cooperation, partnerships, and balance. The shape of the number reflects its vibration. Numbers with a rounded appearance are people-oriented numbers that learn and thrive by interacting with others. These numbers are 2, 3, 5, 6, 8, 9. Numbers composed of straight lines are more mentally oriented and prefer to experience life through the mind and by gathering knowledge. These numbers are 1, 4, 7.

We are now going to calculate numbers to understand our life cycles. When we are calculating numbers to see our weaknesses, or what we lack, we subtract. I want to reinforce that all future events are dependent on the potential of the natal influences. Therefore, in order to gain the most benefit from future readings, we should calculate our natal numerology chart. For a full explanation of how to erect a natal numerology chart, please refer to my previous book *Soul Choices: Six Paths to Find Your Life Purpose.*

The chart below summarizes the general characteristics of each number.

QUALITIES OF NUMBERS

	Positive Qualities	Negative Qualities
1	Authoritative, Ambitious, Independent, Courageous, Pioneering, Aggressive, Dynamic	Domineering, Stubborn, Egotisitcal, Tactless, Selfish
2	Cooperative, Service Oriented, Loving, Considerate, Humble, Patient, Diplomatic	Shy, Vacillating, Cowardly, Wishy-Washy, Oversensative, Indefinite
3	Expressive, Optimistic, Imaginative, Multi-Talented, Social, Creative, Enthusiastic	Vain, Fickle, Scattered, Critical, Egotistical, Jealous, Wasteful
4	Reliable, Conservative, Methodical, Determind, Loyal, Practical, Logical	Dogmatic, Stubborn, Habitual, Rigid, Argumentative, Repressed, Resistant
5	Persuasive, Versatile, Courageous, Passionate, Curious, Futuristic, Adventurous	Overindulgent in the Senses, Unreliable, Inconsistent, Moody, Irresponsible, Careless
6	Caring, Sympathetic, Nurturing, Protective, Domestic, Conscientious, Peace Loving	Self-Righteous, Vain, Sympathetic, Overly Concerned with Others' Affairs

7	Spiritual, Analytical, Withdrawn, Insightful, Philosophical, Introspective, Truth-Seeking	Reclusive, Critical, Cold, Skeptical, Aloof, Lonely
8	Powerful, Money-Conscious, Visionary, Authoritative, Broadminded, Successful, Enterprising	Egotistical, Vain, Power and Money Hungry, Materialistic, Impatient
9	Humanitarian, Idealistic, Brilliant, Creative, Generous, Futuristic, Philanthropic	Egocentric, Impractical, Overemotional, Unconcerned
11	Most intuitive of the numbers, contains all the aspects of 2, plus leadership capabilities. Must learn how to channel intuition without falling off center. Spiritual studies help with balance to reach potential intuitive abilities.	Illogical, Fanatic
22	Most powerful number - master builder - capable of manifesting ideas; can achieve success by combining the intuition of 11 and practicality of 4; grand ideas and leadership ability. Must respond to inner urges and ideas to avoid severe inner conflict.	Impractical, Lazy, Negligent in Developing Talents

Life Class Numbers

Each numerological cycle will trigger us in different ways and areas of life. Let's begin by looking at our Life Class Numbers. Imagine that our life is a school consisting of three classes and one major that leads to a particular degree for this lifetime.

The Life Class Numbers come from our date of birth. Our month, day, and year of birth describe the set of classes or lessons we are learning. Each class is a cycle lasting about twenty-nine years.

First we write our month, day, and year of birth, and then reduce each number to a single digit. We will use October 23, 1965, as our example.

Month $10 = 1$

Day 23 $(2 + 3) = 5$

Year 1965 $(1 + 9 + 6 + 5) = 21$ $(2 + 1) = 3$

Total of the three numbers $(1 + 5 + 3) = 9$

Our first Life Class Number is a 1. From birth to age twenty-nine we are working on building the qualities of this number, such as independence, courage, and assertiveness.

Our second Life Class Number is 5. From age thirty to fifty-nine we are working on building the qualities of curiosity, passion, versatility, and adventure.

Our third Life Class Number is 3. From age sixty until death, we are working on developing our imagination, creativity, self-expression, enthusiasm, and optimism.

When we successfully pass these courses, we will receive our degree in the number 9. If we incorporated the qualities of 1, 3, and 5 into ourselves, then we will be qualified to do the things associated with the 9. For example, we can channel our humanitarian efforts into working for a charity for the homeless. Or we could use our creative energies to support the arts. We can look to the future and see what humanity will need as we move into the next millennium.

Essence Cycles

The essence number is derived from our name and reveals what we are desiring to learn and incorporate into ourselves. The duration of each cycle is different for each person, since it is based on our name. Each Essence number cycle can last anywhere from one to nine years. The longer the essence cycle, the more intense the learning can be since we have a longer period in which to integrate the lesson.

Essence numbers offer us the opportunity to experience deep inner transformation. The more aware we are of the cycle, the better chance we have to cause an internal shift. This number shows us the possibilities and opportunities available to us and where we need to focus our attention. I believe the cycles are always helping us prepare for the next challenge or opportunity. The change of an essence cycle can mirror endings and beginnings in our life.

To calculate our essence number, we need to know the numerical values associated with each letter.

The following chart lists the numerical value of each letter in the alphabet.

1	2	3	4	5	6	7	8	9
A	B	C	D	E	F	G	H	I
J	K	L	M	N	O	P	Q	R
S	T	U	V	W	X	Y	Z	

The first step is to write our full birth name as it appears on our birth certificate, even if we no longer use it, such as in the case of adoptees and married people who assume a spouse's name. Next, assign the correct numerical value to each letter. We will use the example of Sara Anne Dean, who is thirty years old.

$$Sara = 1 + 1 + 9 + 1 = 12$$
$$Anne = 1 + 5 + 5 + 5 = 16$$
$$Dean = 4 + 5 + 1 + 5 = 15$$

The next step is to determine what letter we are at in our name based on our age. In our example, Sara is 30 years old. If Sara equals 12, then we have to repeat the name until we get to 30. We can do two full rounds of her name, which comes to a 24. Then we start back at the first letter S and add 1, and we are at 25. Then we go to the next letter A, and add 1, so we are at 26. Then we go to R, which is 9, so we are at 35. We stop at the letter R because we only need to arrive at 30, her current age. Then we go through the same process for the middle and last name.

Sara = 12 + 12 + (a)1 + (a)1 + r(9) = 35.
We are at the letter r.

Anne = 16 + (a)1 + (n)5 + (n)5 + (e)5 = 32.
We are at the letter e.

Dean = 15 + 15 = 30. We are at the letter n. With Dean, since the letters add up to 15, you just go through his name twice, and stop at n.

Sara = we stop at letter r = 9
Anne = we stop at letter e = 5
Dean = we stop at letter n = 5

Next we add the values of the first, middle, and last names together to arrive at our final Essence number.

(r)9 + (e)5 + (n)5 = 19
Now reduce to a single digit 19 = 1 + 9 = 10 = 1

She is in an Essence cycle #1.

Read below to find the meaning of the Essence numbers.

Essence Cycle Descriptions

1. We are starting a new cycle of personal growth. The universe will offer us opportunities to speak our truth and express our individuality. Since this is a new cycle, we will go through an infancy stage where we are bound to make some mistakes. We must be easy on ourselves as we grow and transform. Expect changes and be courageous. If we use this cycle to develop ourselves and our talents, we can make major accomplishments in the world and emerge as someone who commands respect.

2. This is a cycle where we benefit from listening to our emotions and feelings. We will be more sensitive than usual, so it is helpful to devote time each day for solitude and meditation. We may be more sensitive to our environment and other people. We can act on our inclinations to reach out and help others when we sense they need something. We can build the skills of cooperation, flexibility, and mediation during

this cycle. This is a time to nurture ourselves and our relationships.

3. Now is the time for us to shine! The time is ripe for us to develop our creativity and find a way to uniquely express ourselves. We will be bombarded with events, which will provide us the opportunity to be social and show off our talents. Since our creative energies are at an all-time high, we can make advancements in our career. Watch out for emotional ups and downs during this time. If we can learn to focus, set goals, and control our emotions, this can be a very rewarding essence cycle.

4. This essence cycle is about learning how to build a solid foundation based on hard work. The universe will offer us opportunities to put our talents to use in the work area, so we would be wise to use our resources well. The 4 essence number also asks us to be disciplined in the areas of our health and fitness. Any sense of limitation will most likely be the result of our own thoughts, so we must not let that stop us from plunging ahead with our work. We can learn to appreciate the value of hard work, organization, and dedication to a goal.

5. We will see the power of our charisma during this essence cycle. We can use our beauty and personality to draw us to the people, places, and events that can help boost our career. We should particularly focus on developing our communication skills. It's okay to advertise our strengths to the world, so let's not hide our talents under a bushel basket during this cycle. Overall, we have the opportunity to expand in many areas of our life, so flexibility and adaptability are important. Part of our expansion may come from foreign travel and meeting new people. This is a time of change and action and letting go of old habits and attitudes.

6. This is a loving number that brings family and community to the forefront. We can enjoy time with loved ones and must be prepared to sacrifice some of our personal time to help others in need. We may feel burdened with extra duties, so making time for creative endeavors to offset our workload is important. If we have a flair for creativity, we can excel with the heightened imagination in a 6 essence cycle. We may be more sensitive than usual and will need to strive to maintain balance between our emotions and logic.

7. This is an inward focused cycle, allowing us to concentrate and study esoteric subjects in depth. We may feel the desire to retreat from other people and the outside world, so we must be careful not to become overly reclusive. Our intuition can be heightened, and we would benefit from regular meditations. This is an opportunity to explore our true purpose in the world and to gain a deeper level of self-awareness. Incorporate daily spiritual practices to take advantage of this essence cycle.

8. This essence cycle invites us back out into the world to share our gifts. How do we want to be known in the world? This is our time to become an authority in some aspect of life. Those in the corporate world may advance their careers, while a stay-at-home mom may simply become more authoritative in her parenting style. It is important for us to establish goals and stay focused on our career path. Others will look to us to lead, so we must be willing to step into our power and take on the challenge. Financial issues will be highlighted, so any lessons or beneficial income will be coming our way!

9. This is the culmination of an eight-year period, and our time to take all the wisdom we've built

up and share it generously with others. The universe will give us opportunities to explore our humanitarian side. This is a time to shine our light, help others less fortunate, and serve others. This essence cycle may require us to put our desires on the back burner to help others, but it will be worth it. The time and effort we have put into our own growth will now be available to benefit others as well.

11. Psychic and intuitive experiences are quite common during this essence cycle. We will probably be more sensitive and find our emotions are stronger than usual. We would do well to ground ourselves and balance our mind and heart. Our dreams relay important messages to us, so we would do well to heed their messages. We can be channels for visions from the other side, and the veil between this world and beyond is easier to penetrate in an 11 essence cycle. This is our opportunity to truly deepen into our spiritual nature.

22. This essence cycle allows us to birth ideas and plans that have been ruminating in our minds for many years. The vision we have had finally seems attainable as a map of how to make it happen is now available. We can blend our

practicality and imagination to create something magical. We will most likely need others to help us bring this vision into reality, so it's time for us to gather like-minded folks. This is not the time to be apprehensive, but rather to step into our power. We can do much good for the progress of humanity by bringing something new into the world.

Pinnacle Cycles

The pinnacles are our "guardian angels," offering opportunities to learn and grow. They offer qualities to help us deal with the challenges we face throughout our life.

1. To calculate pinnacle numbers, we will be adding various numbers of our birth date together. Do *not* reduce master numbers.

2. Add the following reduced numbers of your birth:

   a. Day and month for the first pinnacle number

   b. Day and year for the second pinnacle number

c. First and second pinnacles for the third pinnacle number

d. Month and year for the fourth pinnacle number

For example:

1. Write and reduce September 28, 1983, as 9; 28 (2 + 8 = 10; 1 + 0 = 1) = 1; 1983 (1 + 9 + 8 + 3 = 21; 2 + 1 = 3) = 3. Do *not* reduce master numbers. The duration of each Pinnacle number is in parentheses. Month = 9. Day = 1. Year = 3.

2. Add the reduced numbers.

   a. Pinnacle number 1(begins at birth to age 36 minus life path number. Calculate the life path number by adding the month, day and year of birth, and reducing it to a single digit): add day and month: 1 + 9 = 10; 1 + 0 = 1.

   b. Pinnacle number 2 (lasts for nine years): add day and year: 1 + 3 = 4.

   c. Pinnacle number 3 (lasts for nine years): add the first two pinnacles: 1

$+ 4 = 5.$

    d. Pinnacle number 4 (lasts until the end of life): add month and year: $9 + 3 = 12; 1 + 2 = 3.$

Pinnacle Number Descriptions

1.   This is a cycle when you assert your individuality. You will focus on your goals and aspirations to live the life you desire. For success you will need to be assertive, independent, and resilient.

2.   This is a period when your artistic and musical abilities come alive. Your intuition and sensitivity will be heightened. There will be a focus on your personal relationships.

3.   This period is about expansion of your self-expression. You will be drawn to more social events and new creative ways to express yourself.

4.   This is a cycle to get practical and down to work. It is a time to build a foundation and focus on work and family.

5.   This is a fun cycle where you experience the freedom to travel, be adventurous, and let go of

old ways of being. You will need to be flexible to deal with all the change that will be happening. This is an exciting time to take advantage of all the opportunities that come your way.

6. The focus here is on your duty and responsibilities to family and community. Important commitments will be made, including marriage. Your creative and artistic talents will also emerge during this time. You will need to learn to balance your time between family and your own interests.

7. Meditation and contemplation will be especially beneficial during this time. Deep inner focus and concentration will be beneficial to gain the understanding about yourself and the universe needed for your growth. Although you will enjoy being alone during this time, it will be a good balance to share your thoughts and feelings with others.

8. This is a period that requires attention to your work and career. Financial gains are possible if you use your skill at organization, delegation, and leadership.

9. This cycle requires aiding humanity. There will be a need to put aside all selfish and self-serving

desires for the greater good of the world. You will be rewarded spiritually by the service that you provide.

11. Master number. This is a period that allows you to expand your spiritual understandings. Your intuitive abilities can be enhanced, and you will have many important messages to bring to the world. The more you invest in self-growth, the deeper you will be rewarded.

22. Master number. This is the time to manifest your dreams. If you use your practicality and leadership skills, you can make your visions a reality. You will need to commit to your goal and find the appropriate people and resources to make it a reality.

Challenge Numbers

Challenge numbers reveal our weak areas where we will encounter many lessons. Challenges are gifts in disguise because they represent lessons from the universe that can help us evolve. The sooner we are aware of these challenges, the better we'll be able to understand and surmount them.

We encounter four main challenges throughout

our lifetime, each one influencing us at different times. The first challenge begins early in life and continues to approximately age twenty-nine. The second challenge occurs between the ages of thirty to fifty-nine. We feel the most intense challenge, the third one, throughout our entire lifetime. The fourth challenge picks up at age sixty and continues until the end of life.

Calculating Challenge Numbers

Use the following process to calculate challenge numbers. For example, if your birth date is September 28, 1983, write the month, day, and year as single digits. September = 9; 28 = 1 (2 + 8 = 10; 1 + 0 = 1); 1983 = 3 (1 + 9 + 8 + 3 = 21; 2 + 1 = 3). Master numbers are reduced.

Since we will be subtracting numbers here, we will always subtract the smaller number from the larger to avoid a negative number as our answer, which may require us to change the order of the numbers. For example, challenge #1 tells us to subtract month minus day. However, if our day of birth is the larger number, we would flip them around and subtract day minus month.

1. Subtract the month and day (putting the larger number first): 9 − 1 = 8.

2. Subtract the day and year: $3 - 1 = 2$.

3. Subtract the first and second challenge numbers: $8 - 2 = 6$.

4. Subtract the month and year: $9 - 3 = 6$.

Challenge 0

The challenge is to respond to the needs of society. For those having avoided service in the past, there will be many opportunities in this lifetime to serve others in need. Happiness and fulfillment come through service and help to others.

Challenge 1

The challenge is to be independent and self-assertive. For those having too often run with the crowd at the expense of beliefs and values, there will be situations presenting the opportunity to be leaders. These folks need to express their personal views, even if they disagree with those of the majority. The more such people practice independence, self-reliance, and standing up for their beliefs, the happier they will be.

Challenge 2

The challenge is to gain emotional balance by controlling oversensitivity and the tendency to pick up and vicariously experience other people's emotions. The more in touch we are with who we are and the greater the risk we're willing to take in expressing ourselves, the more balanced and centered we become. We need to use intuition and compassion for the benefit of others.

Challenge 3

To build up self-confidence in creative abilities and increase self-worth, we must overcome self-doubt and criticism. The more real we become and the more we express who we are, the easier it will be to relate to other people and feel connected rather than isolated and alone.

Challenge 4

The challenge is to learn organization and to build a foundation one step at a time to achieve success. To achieve success, we must learn practicality and follow through on commitments. Fulfillment will come when we apply the stability of the number 4 to manifest ideas in the physical world.

Challenge 5

The challenge is to stay focused and not to explore every whim and desire for new experiences. We're tempted by many sensual pleasures, so we must learn moderation. We can achieve happiness by learning the value of discipline and the joy of committing to something.

Challenge 6

The challenge is to be more accepting of others, even if they do not quite measure up to our high standards. Opening our minds to include other viewpoints and perspectives will help us be more expansive and accepting. We can also overcome the tendency to be self-righteous by being of service to others through teaching or healing.

Challenge 7

Skepticism and doubt of anything that cannot be logically proved keep us distanced from the spiritual side of life. The challenge is to embrace feelings and intuition and explore the spiritual side of life. There will be opportunities to develop faith. The more we allow faith to break down the barriers to the inner self and emotions, the happier we will be.

Challenge 8

The challenge is to achieve a balance between spiritual and physical goals. When the drive to attain physical wealth and prosperity overshadows spiritual development, happiness will elude us. Until we learn to put our material ambitions into proper perspective, we will be faced with financial challenges. When we master the energies of the number 8, we will understand how to be "in the world but not of it."

Personal Year Cycle

What steps should we take to fulfill our life purpose? How do we know when it is time to act or to sit back and formulate a plan? Which lessons should we focus on now? Our lives run in cycles of nine years. Each year brings its own energies, influences, and lessons. A cycle begins with a personal year 1, indicating new beginnings where we foster new ideas. The cycle ends with year 9, the year of completion and transformation as we assimilate all that we've built during the last eight years.

Personal Year Number

To calculate your personal year, add the day and month of your birth to the current year. For example, for the year 2020, a person born on March 3 would calculate his personal year as follows.

1. Add March: 3

2. Add day of birth: 3

3. Add the numbers in the current year:
   $$2020 = 2 + 0 + 2 + 0 = 4.$$

4. Add the results: $3 + 3 + 4 = 10 = 1 + 0 = 1.$

In 2020, a person born on March 3 would be in a personal year 1.

The following summarizes the energies of each year. For additional insight, study the Qualities of Numbers Chart earlier in this chapter.

Year 1: Set new ideas into motion, make changes, and embark on a new direction.

Year 2: Build important relationships and develop ideas started in year 1.

Year 3: Add creativity to the ideas started in year 1.

Year 4: Work hard and stay disciplined to achieve results.

Year 5: Adapt an attitude of freedom and expectancy: this is a year of unpredictability.

Year 6: Serve and practice responsibility.

Year 7: Pursue spiritual study and personal growth.

Year 8: Reap the benefits of efforts and gain recognition for accomplishments.

Year 9: Complete all that has transpired over the last eight years. Let go of what no longer serves. Prepare to start fresh in year 1.

Activities

1. Calculate your Life Class Numbers. Focus on your current life class based on your age, and write down the qualities you desire to build. Include details on how you will build these qualities within.

2. Calculate your current Essence cycle. Brainstorm ways you can develop the qualities related to this number. If you have already been in this cycle for a while, do some reflective writing about how you experienced this number.

3. Calculate your four pinnacle numbers. Write how you will use the current pinnacle number in your life to help you.

4. Calculate your four challenge numbers. Reflect on the challenges you experienced that are related to your current challenge number. Brainstorm ways you can deal

with possible future challenges related to challenge #3.

5. Calculate your personal year number for this year. Brainstorm what actions to take this year that would support the energies of that number.

Chapter 16
Astrology Is God's Timing

Time is the wisest counselor of all.
—Pericles

Astrology is a precise tool that guides us toward self-awareness. It is based on the principal "As above, so below." Planetary patterns correspond to and reflect cycles and patterns on Earth. Souls choose their time of birth to correspond to favorable planetary influences that will help them learn lessons and fulfill their karmic destiny. In this chapter we will explore how the movement of the planets triggers us to grow and evolve. We will explore universal astrological events that affect everyone at the same time, as well as individual events that are particular to each person's individual chart. We will explore wake-up calls from Saturn and our urge for freedom with Uranus. We will explore how Neptune opens up our spirituality, Pluto drives us to use our power for good, and Jupiter broadens our horizons. The South Node reveals where we are meeting our past, and the North Node reveals where we need to grow. Lastly, we will explore the cycles that affect our love life, career, spirituality, education, and transformation. The cycles are a blueprint for the unfoldment of our lives.

We are born with a particular planetary configuration, known as our horoscope (a representational map of the sky, based on a particular date, time, and place of birth). However, the planets are always moving, and their movement stirs things up on our natal chart, often throwing us into a crisis. This crisis will cause us to look within and hopefully change and grow. We can prepare ourselves for these crises by watching the planets as they move, noting when they will trigger one of our natal planets. When people want to know when they will get married, or find a new job, or heal from a sickness, astrology can help us find these answers, because I believe astrology is God's timing. The Creator blessed us with the planets so we could understand the cycles of our lives. Let's look at the purpose of each planet to better understand the meaning of the cycles. We will begin with the Sun and Moon, which technically aren't planets, and are more akin to celestial bodies.

Sun

The Sun represents how we want to be recognized, our creative urge, and how we express our creativity. The placement of the Sun is crucial to understanding our life purpose because it is the most influential planet on our chart.

Purpose: To understand our basic character.

Moon

The Moon represents our emotional nature, revealing how we nurture others and how we want to be nurtured. It also focuses on our domestic life, how we behave within a family, and how we relate to a nurturing person growing up (usually our mother). It represents our urge for security and reveals how we create a "nest" for ourselves. The Moon also reveals our feelings and sensitivities.

Purpose: To understand our feelings and emotions.

Mercury

Mercury is the Roman god of commerce, eloquence, travel, cunning, and theft who served as messenger to the other gods.[1] The planet Mercury relates to the mind, revealing the way we think and communicate. Depending on what sign of the zodiac Mercury is in (i.e., what sign influences Mercury, determined by planetary alignment), this planet reveals what we focus our mental abilities on, be it wealth, service, or other avenues, as well as what piques our curiosity.

Purpose: To communicate and develop our mental abilities.

Venus

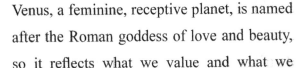 Venus, a feminine, receptive planet, is named after the Roman goddess of love and beauty, so it reflects what we value and what we regard as beautiful. This planet reveals our sensual nature and what we see as pleasurable and joyful. It shows how we behave in intimate relationships and how we express love and affection. Venus governs marriage, appreciation, and our social natures.

Purpose: To learn to receive love and understand the essence of harmony.

---

1   Definitions of the gods' names are from *Merriam Webster's Collegiate Dictionary, Tenth Edition* (Springfield, MA: Merriam-Webster, 1993).

Mars

Mars is the aggressive, male counterpart of Venus. In Roman mythology, Mars was the god of war. Mars represents how we initiate and take action and how we assert ourselves. Therefore, when we repress this Mars quality, we often become ill. We must work with the Mars energy to promote healthy self-expression. In love, Mars represents our sexual drive. It also represents the areas and ways in which we will be ambitious.

Purpose: To understand how to direct energy to manifest our desires.

Jupiter

Jupiter is the chief Roman god, the god of light, the sky, and weather. This planet deals with expansion, travel, luck, and opportunities. It reveals the avenues through which we receive monetary benefits and rewards from good deeds done in the past. It shows how we share our talents and generosity with others. Jupiter reveals the areas in which our optimism shines and where we hold hope and high aspirations.

Purpose: To learn to cause prosperity, abundance, and expansion in all areas of life.

Saturn

In Roman mythology, Saturn is the god of agriculture. Saturn is the planet of maturity and responsibility. Therefore, the sign in which it appears indicates the particular areas we need to develop. Saturn continually brings us lessons in these areas and is a strong driving force in our karma, helping us to see the cause and effect of our actions. Saturn is where we experience many challenges and limitations until we master the Saturn lessons. It indicates what types of work and responsibilities we take on and how we handle those responsibilities. Since Saturn represents what we lack, we may feel very insecure in this area.

Purpose: To learn responsibility, discipline, and respect structure.

The three planets that follow are the "outer" or "generational" planets. They can affect an entire generation due to their slow movement through the signs, which may account for similarities in thought among generations. These planets do not affect us as much on a personal level as do the previous planets, Sun and Moon. As Saturn provides a constant stimulus to mature in a certain area, Uranus, Neptune, and Pluto provide a constant stimulus to go beyond the ordinary and reach for transcendence. The energies of these planets can lead us down the dark road of escapism, rebelliousness, and radical negative behaviors, or toward new, more positive ways of being, thinking, and expressing ourselves. The entire consciousness of a generation can change when we harness the energy of these planets.

Uranus

In Greek mythology, Uranus is the sky personified as a god and father of the Titans, a family of giants. This planet brings us the energies of independence, change, and uniqueness. To make the best use of these energies—which can come upon us quite suddenly—we must listen to our intuition so that we are open to the flashes of insight that Uranus brings. The Uranus energy is often experienced as a desire for freedom and a desire to be different. Thus, we need to move forward and experiment with our ideas. The sign Uranus is in reveals the nature of the experimentation. When people attune themselves to the vibration of Uranus, they can use these new ideas and innovative thoughts to change old ways of being and thinking.

Purpose: To learn to cause change by using intuition.

Neptune

Neptune is the Roman god of the sea. Its purpose is for us to connect with our soul and the spiritual world. Neptune ignites our awareness of other worlds and higher states of consciousness. It is often associated with the part of us that wants to be swept away or to see only the rosy part of life rather than reality. Neptune shows how we are inspired to transcend the physical, perhaps through art or religion or with drugs and alcohol. Neptune reveals where we lack clear perception and where we place our faith. This planet rules illusions, delusion, and spirituality. It reveals how we deceive others and ourselves. We may have to sacrifice attachment to find the "ultimate" here on Earth and realize it is only through higher spiritual ideals that the energies of Neptune can help us move toward ultimate fulfillment.

Purpose: To transcend the mundane physical world and reach for higher states of awareness.

Pluto

Another Greek god is Pluto, the god of the underworld. Pluto is the planet of regeneration and transformation: death and rebirth. It brings to the forefront desires from the past that must be elevated. We can transform ourselves using Pluto's drive to delve into understanding others and ourselves at the core level. We can use the concentrated Plutonian power to advance positive energies, such as honesty and love, or to regress by using negative energies, such as deception and cruelty. Focusing on our spiritual nature moves us beyond the pairs of opposites to find balance and understanding. We can use Pluto's power to wipe out the old, much of which is karma from past lives, and bring in the new, which will open doors to new ways of being and to tremendous growth for future generations.

Purpose: To transform lower energies and emotions into a higher vibration.

Triggers

A planet triggers another planet by the way it aspects it. The type of aspect reveals how we will experience the trigger. Aspects are the angular measurement between two planets. Harmonious aspects show where we will experience ease and perhaps fortunate events. Challenging aspects reveal areas where we will experience difficulty and tension. These are areas we have not fully developed and, therefore, are lessons we need to learn. Neutral aspects are neither good nor bad.

Some of the most important aspects are the

harmonious aspects (sextile and trine), challenging aspects (opposition and square), and neutral aspect (conjunction).

Harmonious Aspects

The harmonious aspects are those that come easily. The most significant harmonious aspects include sextiles and trines.

There is not much tension involved with planets that are in harmonious aspect, so the potential for growth is not as great as with challenging aspects. Harmonious aspects reveal what we have already developed in past lives, so not much effort is required to bring them out. We simply need to tap into these skills and use them to fulfill our current life purpose.

Sextile

This occurs when two planets are 60 degrees (two signs) apart, which enhances their ability to complement each other. This cooperation makes it easy to learn something new; combining the two energies creates a pathway for opportunities. Possible sextile combinations are these: fire and air signs, and earth and water signs.

Trine

This occurs when two planets are 120 degrees (four signs)

apart. There is a harmonious flow of energy between the planets, indicating skills, talents, and abilities that come easily. Sometimes this can result in laziness as we fall into the least line of resistance. A grand trine is made up of three planets in the same element (fire, earth, air, water), each about 120 degrees apart.

Challenging Aspects

The most significant challenging aspects are oppositions (180 degrees) and squares (90 degrees). Contrary to what many people believe, these challenging aspects are not always bad. In fact, due to the tension they provoke within a person, they offer the most opportunity for growth. The conflict acts as a stimulus to reach a resolution. It is during this process that tremendous growth can occur. The degree of transformation that can be achieved equals the amount of effort the individual puts into it.

Opposition

This occurs when there are two opposing factors that can be harmonized by incorporating a balance between the two opposing polarities. There is a polarization between two signs, such as Aries (exclusiveness) and Libra (inclusiveness). The key is to be aware of and find balance between the two.

Square

A square aspect represents a conflict, or competition and challenge. When the challenge is understood, it can be a major step forward in growth. The planets that square each other have different purposes and thus interfere with each other's expression. The challenge is to create cooperation between these two forces by understanding both energies and with skill blending them into harmony. The Sun represents personality and the Moon emotions. For example, when the Sun "squares" the Moon, the result is that the head says one thing and the heart says another. We need to understand how to blend thinking and feeling. Until then, we will be blocked and frustrated.

Neutral Aspects

A neutral aspect is neither favorable nor unfavorable. The effect depends upon the planets involved and how the person works with them.

Conjunction

A conjunction involves two to three planets all within an orb of seven degrees. There is an intensification of themes from the planets involved in the conjunction. The planets will usually reside in the same zodiac sign and intensify each other's energy. A conjunction manifests a strong need or emphasis within an area of a person's life.

Planets also trigger areas of our lives when they transit a particular zodiac house. Let's explore the houses. Houses are divisions of space based on Earth's twenty-four-hour rotation. Houses describe where the influences enter into a person's life. Each house is influenced by a particular zodiac sign, as well as the planet or planets that rule the sign. The houses have no life of their own. Rather, the house creates the stage on which a particular planet and sign will express itself. The cusp separates one house from another. The zodiac sign on the cusp influences the energy of the house. For example, if Gemini is on the cusp of the seventh house of partnership and marriage, communication will be an important factor in our relationships with others.

Houses indicate the areas in which our karmic lessons will play out. If we have several planets in a particular house, many of our experiences will be focused in that area. If someone has no planets in a house, that area of life is not a strong influence that the person wanted or needed in life.

Houses one through six relate to the self. Each one builds upon the next, so as we progress through each house, we develop qualities that help us move to the next house or area of life. The progression through the houses allows us to add understandings in many different areas:

1. We establish our self-identity.

2. Once we know ourselves, we can accumulate resources.

3. We develop mental capabilities to use our resources.

4. With a developed mind and plenty of resources we are now ready to establish a foundation that will become our home.

5. With a secure home foundation, we can focus on the development of our creativity.

6. We have built enough within ourselves to share our wisdom and time with the world through some form of service.

The following descriptions list the sign and planetary rulers for each house.

First House (Aries; Mars)

The first house has the qualities of Aries: initiative, new beginnings, self-expression, courage, and action. This house is about identity and revealing personality and expression. It reveals our approach to life and how we see the world. The cusp (a line that separates one house from the next) of the first house is called the "ascendant."

Second House (Taurus; Venus)

This is the house of comfort and security. It deals with the acquisition of physical resources, financial matters, and how we establish security. It also reveals how we gauge our self-worth and value.

Third House (Gemini; Mercury)

This is the house of communication and the mind. It deals with the processing and assimilation of information, perception, and logic. Since an air sign resides here, there is a heavy focus on the workings of the mind, particularly on the discrimination process. It carries the Gemini qualities of curiosity, adaptability, and versatility.

Fourth House (Cancer; Moon)

This house is concerned with security and the home. It reveals information about the nature of the home and the family we grew up with, as well as the type of dwelling we will create for ourselves when we mature. It reveals our roots and how we use our nurturing and protective qualities.

Fifth House (Leo; Sun)

This is the house of creativity. The Leo qualities of self-expression and love are channeled through this house. Activities related to travel, adventure, love affairs, children, teaching, and the performing arts are emphasized in this house. It shows how we express joy and vitality.

Sixth House (Virgo; Mercury)

This house is the house of duty, concerned with attitudes toward work, service, and health/hygiene-related issues. How we view work and the type of work we choose is shown here. Since it is ruled by Mercury, this house deals with mental analysis and discrimination.

Houses seven through twelve show how we relate to other people and interact with individuals and groups. It shows how we express tendencies of the opposite house with other individuals. For example, the seventh house is opposite the first house, the eighth house is opposite the second house, and so on. If the first house reveals how we express our individuality, then the seventh house shows how we harmonize and relate to others.

Seventh House (Libra; Venus)

This is the partnership house dealing with unions of all kinds, such as marriage, friendships, and business partnerships. Its ruler, Venus, brings out what we value as beautiful and our ideas about love. This house reveals the nature of the mates we attract and our ideas about marriage. This house is about Libra's quest for cooperation and balance.

Eighth House (Scorpio; Pluto)

This is the opposite of the second house, so it deals with how we handle financial resources with family and partners. It concerns money matters including wills, taxes, inheritances, trusts, and money accumulated in partnerships and business ventures. Due to the influence of Scorpio and Pluto, there is an interest in the occult, death, sexuality, regeneration, and transformation.

Ninth House (Sagittarius; Jupiter)

In contrast to what one personally thinks, as revealed in the third house, the ninth house shows the thinking of a collective group consciousness reflected in philosophy, religion, legal systems, science, psychology, and teachings of higher education. The expansion and inspiration from Jupiter help us tap into a collective consciousness to see the needs of society. Travel is also associated with this house.

Tenth House (Capricorn; Saturn)

This house deals with how we use our ambitions and into what professional/career arena we channel these ambitions. It reveals our responsibilities to the world and the reputation we build for ourselves. It reveals how we respond to authorities, law, government, and other business systems.

Eleventh House (Aquarius; Uranus)

This house is about social consciousness. It shows how we express our creativity within a group, as opposed to the individual creativity expressed in the opposite fifth house. It focuses on how we relate to people outside of intimate relationships. The influence of Aquarius here is interested in humanitarian concerns on a large scale and how groups of people work together to achieve some ideal that will minister to humanity at large.

Twelfth House (Pisces; Neptune)

The twelfth house uncovers hidden thoughts and behaviors. It reveals patterns and habits. It also reveals our karma. Therefore, it stores what we try to hide: those unconscious drives we are not even aware of. To work with this house, we must face both karma and unconscious behaviors. It deals with the psychological and physical health of a culture, and is, therefore, concerned with group health organizations such as mental institutions, ashrams, and hospitals. The influence of Neptune here can cause us to deceive ourselves or cloud our perception of reality. There is also the possibility of developing artistic talents and compassion for those less fortunate by drawing on the Piscean energy that occupies this house.

Universal Astrological Events

Now we will explore the various astrological events. I want to reinforce that all future events are dependent on the potential of the natal influences. Therefore, in order to gain the most benefit from future readings, we need to understand our natal astrology chart. For a full explanation of how to understand a natal chart, please refer to my book *Soul Choices: Six Paths to Find Your Life Purpose, or schedule an astrology reading at www. intuitiveschool.com.*

In astrology there are certain universal planetary events that affect everyone at the same age and have the potential to bring about great transformation. Then we have individual events, which occur at unique time periods for each person. These events occur when transiting (moving) planets make an aspect to one of our natal planets, triggering us in some way. Harmonious aspects allow us to highlight our talents or take advantage of opportunities, whereas challenging aspects reveal where we will experience difficulty and tension. A neutral aspect, such as a conjunction, is when two planets are in the same zodiac sign and so close in degrees that they touch each other. When two planets conjunct each other, their combined energy creates intensity and power.

Saturn Return

The most significant universal event we will explore is the Saturn return. This occurs for everyone at the age of twenty-nine and a half, which is the time it takes Saturn to make a complete revolution around the astrology chart back to its natal position. This event is meant to get us disciplined and wake us up to our life purpose. Saturn is like a parent, helping us mature into adults. Saturn highlights where we have been irresponsible and brings opportunities for us to rectify this. Up until the return, Saturn gives us gentle nudges, but if we still are off course, then the nudges become stronger pushes during the return.

To get a deeper understanding of how our Saturn

return will affect us, it is necessary to study its placement on our astrology chart. We take into account the house and sign position of Saturn and the aspects it makes to other planets to fully grasp the calling and possible challenges of our Saturn return. The basic question that Saturn asks of us is, "Will we answer the calling?"

The Saturn return lasts for about two and a half years, allowing us ample time to obtain what we desire. This event is not only a time where we will be challenged and put to the test, but also a time where doors will open. I describe this period in our life as a tidal wave. If we face our responsibilities and make strides toward fulfilling our life purpose, we can reap the rewards. If we do it right, we have the next twenty-nine years, until the second Saturn return at age fifty-nine, to live a joyful and purposeful existence.

However, if we choose to ignore our inner calling and avoid opportunities that present themselves, we will probably get sucked under the wave and feel overwhelmed. The tidal wave of opportunities lessens after the age of thirty-one, so it's in our best interest to ride the wave when it presents itself.

Saturn demands that we be responsible for both our outer as well as inner needs. It is a period where we need to fulfill our financial, job, and family duties. We also need to be responsible for our mental and emotional needs, such as using our creativity and engaging in meaningful relationships. If we have been talking about wanting to be a famous soccer player ever since we were ten years old, but have done nothing to obtain that desire, then during the Saturn return we will begin to feel a lot of pressure to either go after that dream or do something else. Anything that is not in alignment with our highest good will begin to feel like a limitation that aggravates us to do something.

The Saturn return is a period in our lives where we need to critically look at everything in our lives, from the people we associate with, to our job and hobbies, and discard those things which do not serve our purpose. This is why many people get divorced, leave jobs, and move to new locations. Therefore, I urge people to wait to get married until after their Saturn return. We go through so much inner transformation that a marriage often cannot withstand the changes. However, for those couples that are mature and have found a common life purpose, this period is an opportunity to deepen their relationship. Some marriages become stronger as a result, and couples often find they are ready to have children at this time.

For those of us who have found our calling early in life, Saturn also helps us to harvest the fruits of our actions. Our work dedication may pay off in the form of a promotion or salary increase. Our status in the community may grow, and we may be seen as an expert in our particular field of work.

Saturn gives us a second chance, when it makes its second return at age fifty-nine. The same process occurs again, but due to our age difference, we experience this period much differently. Most of us will not be having children or starting a new career at this age, so the second return is more of an inner maturation and a time to give back. If we have lived our life in alignment with our purpose, we have most likely gained wisdom which Saturn urges us to share with humanity. Some people may respond to this by writing a book, while others may volunteer to work with those less fortunate. Our wisdom may attract the younger generation in search of guidance. Therefore, working with the youth in some capacity is a great way to live up to Saturn's demands on us.

For those of us who have squandered our middle years and have done nothing to be responsible or live according to our life purpose, then the second Saturn return can be quite uncomfortable. We find we have nothing to give back to humanity, and feel a sense of disappointment that we have wasted so much time. This may lead us to become the "grouchy old person."

Uranus Opposition

As we read in the above description of Uranus, this is a planet that helps us fight the urge to go with the herd mentality. Uranus urges us to bring out our uniqueness and do what is right for us, regardless of what others want us to do. When transiting Uranus opposes our natal Uranus, this is known as the Uranus opposition, occurring about the age of forty. This astrological event is often what triggers a midlife crisis for many. Uranus urges us to be free, so anything that is inhibiting us to live our life the way we want becomes intolerable. How we respond to these limitations varies according to our level of maturity and self-awareness. Some adults may adopt the "screw it" mentality and ditch their responsibilities. This might include quitting their job, leaving their marriage, and heading to Mexico! Although this may bring a temporary feeling of freedom, it doesn't really get to the core of what the Uranus opposition is all about.

The message of Uranus is deeper. It wants us to find a way to bring out our unique essence. It is a time to do some soul searching and find out what that is. If we get honest with ourselves, most of us had a clue what that was when we were in our early twenties, or we figured it out during the Saturn return. If we didn't respond then, Uranus makes it easier for us to do so now. It is common for many people to go back to school and study what they really wanted to do when they attended college in their twenties. The Uranus opposition requires us to be a bit selfish in order to pursue our unique interest. Hopefully we have built up a supportive group of people that will help us fulfill our Uranian urges to be different.

The pressure to conform and please our parents is typically stronger in our early years than when we are forty. Therefore, many of the choices we made in those early years were often the result of this pressure to conform. Depending on the level of societal and familial influence, some of us married partners because they were seen by our family and others as a good choice, rather than out of love. Likewise, our early career choices often reflected the need for parental approval, or to feel accepted by society, and didn't reflect our inner desires. The Uranus return is an opportunity to break free from those ties and create new ones that reflect our true self.

To get a deeper understanding of how our Uranus opposition will affect us, it is necessary to study its placement on our astrology chart. We take into account the house and sign position of Uranus, and the aspects it makes to other planets, to fully grasp the calling and possible challenges of our Uranus opposition. An in-depth understanding of our natal Uranus will also help us to know where we want to leave our unique mark on the world. It shows us where we want to deviate from the herd and do something different. The question that Uranus wants us to answer is "how will we leave our unique footprint in the world?"

Uranian Wake-Up Calls

Uranus gives us some smaller wake-up calls to prepare us for the opposition. At age fourteen, Uranus forms a waxing sextile. This event corresponds with the onset of puberty, when we experience the desire for freedom! This is the age when we slowly begin to separate from our home and family. Depending on the child, it may be something as simple as beginning to spend more time with friends as opposed to family. A more independent type personality may completely withdraw from the family and begin acting out in various rebellious ways. We can see this Uranian energy in middle school students, who are often challenging to teach.

Seven years later at approximately age twenty-one, we experience a Uranus waxing square. Since most of us have flown the coop by this age, our urge to be free from limitations is now directed toward society. We can respond to this in several ways. A positive response would be to allow our eccentricity to flower and be our unique self. If we are not strong enough, we will cave in and follow the herd. Another response is to rebel against societal laws and become criminals. Ultimately this will lead to possible imprisonment, exactly the thing that Uranus was trying to avoid! Marriage during this period can prove problematic since it is a time in our life where Uranus asks us to discover our unique talents and beliefs rather than compromising ourselves for the sake of blending our values with another.

Uranus awakens us once again at age sixty-three, when we experience a waning square. A square is a challenging aspect, so we will definitely feel the tension. This coincides with the time that many of us decide to retire from our career if it doesn't align with our purpose, or find one that better suits us. For those of us who felt limited by our career, it is a liberating time to be able to retire. However, Uranus wouldn't be happy if we went into a nursing home where we would feel like we were being discarded by society. One way we can answer the challenge of shining our light in the world is to channel our talents into various hobbies and find ways to share our gifts with others in the form of volunteering. If we have been responsible with our finances up to this point, we can afford to leave our job and focus our efforts on giving back to humanity.

By the time we reach the age of sixty, many of us have released the need to please others. Without the temptation to please our bosses, parents, or partners, we are free to be our authentic self. We can thank Uranus for the ability to say "bug off" to those that want us to conform.

Our Spiritual Wake-Up Call

Neptune is the planet that wakes us up to our true nature as spirit and reminds us that there is more to life than what we see with our physical eyes. Neptune inspires us to see the good in others and the world. In its attempt to illuminate the darkness of evil, it sometimes blinds us to it. When reality is too grim, we may choose to look the other way, and then we risk getting the wool pulled over our eyes.

Our first wake-up call occurs at approximately age twenty-eight, when it makes a sextile to our natal Neptune. This creates an opportunity to recognize and cultivate our spirituality. There are many ways we could respond to the recognition that we are spiritual beings living in a material world. Some of us may realize the religion we were raised with no longer nourishes our soul, and we seek something deeper. A productive response to the Neptune wake-up call is to explore metaphysical paths that teach us the mysteries of the world. The mystical sciences rather than intellectual concepts can be appropriate answers to the wake-up call.

For some of us it is frightening to realize what we thought was real is not! When our reality shatters, we may become unbalanced and need counseling.

Neptune urges us to explore beyond the drudgery of everyday life. If there are no spiritual or metaphysical paths that present themselves, we may seek other ways to escape our physical reality through drugs or alcohol.

Neptune triggers another spiritual crisis at approximately age forty-one. This waxing square can be the beginning to a "midlife crisis" for some of us. The square causes friction, making us question our faith. We no longer want to blindly follow, but seek a direct experience with the divine through practices such as meditation, chanting, devotional prayer, or a spiritual pilgrimage. Our response to this test of faith depends a great deal on our previous religious or spiritual training.

Neptune begins to prepare us for our death, when it opposes our natal Neptune at about age eighty-three. By this age many of us are facing the reality that we are mortal beings and our time on planet Earth is limited. We begin to question what will happen after death, and Neptune reminds us that our true self is immortal and will continue to exist after our physical death. However, if we ignore Neptune's message, we may become fearful of death and anxious of our impending transition. If we follow Neptune's direction to engage in spiritual practices, our transition back to the spirit world will be a pleasant journey. Neptune is the link to our memory of our time in other places such as Atlantis and the astral plane.

Our Power Drive

Pluto is the planet that triggers us to use our power to transform ourselves and the world. Pluto will trigger us in whatever way is necessary for us to change, evolve, and grow. If there is something standing in the way of our growth, Pluto will find a way to clear it away. Whatever we lose is usually something we have become too obsessed with. The more attached we are to a person, job, or way of life, the harder it will be when we lose. it. We can make the transition easier when we realize nothing in the physical is permanent, and so letting go is the productive way to respond to a Plutonian astrological event. When Pluto clears away the old, a space is created for something new and better to replace it.

The timing of Pluto's first trigger, a sextile to one of our natal planets, is different for each person. This opportunistic aspect motivates us to use our power to do something worthwhile in the world. Since Pluto rules

Scorpio, it fires up our energy and helps us get in touch with our power. Our feelings about power determine to a great extent how we will respond to this event. If we can't channel this intense power to create something, we may use it for destruction. As Einstein taught us, energy cannot be created or destroyed, only changed.

The next important Plutonian cycle is a waxing square. Again, the timing is different for each person. The tension caused by the square, coupled with the intense nature of Pluto, creates a recipe for positive transformation or destruction. The area of tension will be experienced in the house position of Pluto. A careful investigation of Pluto's zodiac placement will help us understand the way we will approach and respond to the tension. One strategy is to release any Plutonian compulsions by focusing our energies in the opposite house and sign of our natal Pluto. For example, if our natal Pluto is in Taurus in the fifth house, our tendency might be to obsess over our creations. Therefore, by refocusing our energies in the eleventh house, we could channel our abilities into helping other groups and organizations and being of service to humanity. Our creative abilities would no longer just be for our own enjoyment, but rather for the good of humanity.

The Call to Broaden Our Horizons

Most of us enjoy answering Jupiter's wake-up calls, since they normally bring us great benefits. If we put in effort, we can walk hand in hand with Jupiter into a world of abundance. Jupiter triggers to our natal planets typically bring opportunities that can broaden our minds and hearts, increase our pocketbooks, and connect us with foreign lands and people. Wherever in our life we have put in effort, Jupiter can bring us the prize. This is exactly what can happen during a cherished Jupiter return. During this return when Jupiter conjuncts our natal Jupiter, the energy is heightened and opportunities abound. To know where these possibilities exist, we need to look at the zodiac sign and house location of Jupiter. For example, if Jupiter is posited in the tenth house, we have the potential to improve our work situation in the form of a promotion or salary increase. A Jupiter conjunction in the second house can help us increase our financial stability and acquire more assets.

Since Jupiter is about abundance, there is always the possibility of overdoing it. Jupiter makes us feel so confident that we might overextend ourselves by biting off more than we can chew. A Jupiter conjunction in the sixth house can lead to excessive eating, leading to weight gain. Jupiter in the fifth house might lead to excessive partying or gambling.

Our Timeline from the Past to the Future

The nodes give us a clear distinction between our past and our future. Imagine a timeline that begins with the South Node and ends with the North Node. It is a timeline of our past and future. In other words, we came from the South Node where we lived our past life and are moving toward the sign of the North Node in the present life. Another way of looking at the South Node is that it reveals our karma, and the North Node reveals the way to resolve the karma. The South Node shows what qualities and personality behaviors have already been developed and the North Node shows what needs to be developed. The nodes are opposites, so the farther we walk away from the South Node and toward the North Node, we can balance these polar opposites.

The South Node represents all the understandings and experiences from past lives and reveals things that come easily to us. Because South Node patterns are so ingrained in us, this behavior is sometimes unconscious and habitual. We must use the South Node productively by letting go of negative patterns and habits, and use the positive qualities built in the past to help others.

To go beyond the limitations of the past we need to move toward the North Node. It always resides in the sign and house opposite the South Node. By embracing the opposite qualities of the North Node, we overcome the limitations of the South Node. The North Node reveals the qualities and understandings we need to develop during this lifetime. Since the North Node points to the future and contains behaviors not yet encountered, it may be a challenge, at first, to work with these new factors. Some people may experience fear at stepping into what the North Node offers simply because it is new. We must embrace the curiosity that leads to this virgin territory, which encompasses the major lessons to be learned by the soul during this lifetime. To master these lessons and fully assimilate new behaviors requires awareness, diligence, patience, and courage.

The nodes are like two magnets pulling us in different directions. The South Node pulls us to the old, familiar past behaviors. The North Node pulls us away from the old behaviors to new territory and areas we have not yet explored. It is the excitement of what lies in the unknown that is the impetus for us to embrace the North Node. The key to working with the polarity created by the North and South Nodes is to use the past understandings and strengths (South Node) as a foundation to move forward with awareness and curiosity (North Node) and incorporating the lessons of this new area slowly and with compassion for the self. We need to balance these two qualities in order to stabilize our life. The way to integrate the North and South Nodes is through the Moon. Examine the sign and house position of your Moon to see how it can help with this process.

These nodes are important triggers for understanding our past and responding to our future. The house where the transiting or progressed South Node enters is where we meet our past. The South Node reminds us that we cannot run and hide from our past because it will always come back to haunt us. Our past may greet us in the form of a person, such as an unrequited love from a past life. Or it may appear as habits and patterns that we haven't dealt with. The South Node is our storehouse of all the gifts and talents we have built in past lives. It is a foundation of skills we can use to help others and to make the world a better place. It is what we already know, so it won't help us grow in this lifetime, but this wisdom can be used to help others.

When the transiting North Node triggers a point on our astrology chart, it signals where we need to grow and expand. We then need to look at the house and sign of the transiting North Node to learn more about the nature of the evolutionary step that we need to explore. Taking this step is not always comfortable or enjoyable, but it is necessary for us to grow.

Our Unique Plan for Unfoldment

Now we'll explore various astrological events that will occur for everyone at different times. These events reveal when and how your life will most likely unfold. In order to forecast these future events, we study the movement of planets as they transit (move) through an individual's astrology chart. We look at the sign and house position of the transiting planet, and any aspects it makes to our natal planets to understand the nature of the trigger.

Love and Beauty with Venus and Mars

Many of us want to know when love will come knocking at our door. We can look to Venus, Jupiter, and Mars to get some clues as to when we will be triggered to reach out and explore intimacy. Venus, the planet of love, beauty, and harmony, can wake us up to love. When transiting Venus enters our fifth house, we may find a new romance, or feel compelled to create something beautiful. Venus urges us to deepen our connection with our children. It is a good time to plan fun activities where our own childlike self can come out and play! When Venus enters our seventh house, the romantic love that began in the fifth house may mature into marriage. Venus in the seventh house reminds us to appreciate all our intimate connections, from business alliances to our best friends.

The potential for love and artistic beauty is also ignited when transiting Venus conjuncts our natal Sun. We may fall in love with our ideal partner, or we may learn to love ourselves more! It is a time to appreciate the journey we have walked so far and to create something beautiful. This is a great time for a family reunion or having a family portrait painted. It would feel good to indulge in creative endeavors of any type when Venus hits our Sun. We should heed any grand creative ideas that come to us during this Venus-Sun conjunction because they have the potential to be amazing!

Transiting Venus conjunct our natal Mars, or vice versa, arouses our sexuality, giving us the drive to go out and find a partner. We may be more inclined to engage in social activities, or even try online dating. Whatever bonds we form under this aspect will most likely have an underlying sexual drive.

When Venus goes retrograde, it is a time to go within and reflect on our intimate relationships. This occurs when the Earth passes an outer planet that is moving more slowly or when an inner planet passes the Earth. Retrograde planets cause us to go deeply inward, allowing us to gain understandings related to the planet. Once the lessons have been learned, the planet can express in a powerful way. We can heal past wounds and complete unfinished business with people. Then when Venus goes direct, we can approach our intimate relationships with a fresh attitude.

Another relationship trigger is when a transiting planet makes an aspect to the planetary rulers of the fifth and seventh houses. For example, suppose Pisces is on the seventh house cusp, and the ruler Neptune is in my eighth house. If transiting Pluto conjuncts my natal Neptune, this could signal an ending (eighth house in Pluto signals endings) to a marriage. Another example is a chart with Gemini on the fifth house cusp and its ruler Mercury in the ninth house. If transiting Jupiter conjuncts my natal Mercury, I may start a romance with a person from another country. (Ninth house rules foreigners and the fifth house rules romance. Mercury encourages social activity.)

Jupiter can bring us abundance in love when it transits our fifth and seventh houses. When it transits the fifth house it can be the beginning of a wonderful courtship, followed by a potential marriage when it moves to our seventh house.

When transiting Jupiter makes a favorable aspect to our natal Venus, we can expect all our relationships to grow and new opportunities for love. We can also be inspired to create beauty in our lives through artistic avenues.

Emotions and Nurturing with the Progressed Moon

The transiting Moon moves quickly, remaining only about two and a half days in each zodiac sign and house. This is too quick to lead to any major events, so we look to the slower moving progressed Moon to see possible relationship information. The progressed Moon reveals where our heart is centered. Therefore, when it passes through the fifth or seventh house, our heart is focused on emotional connection and intimate partnerships. Our craving for deep intimacy helps us move beyond superficial communication. As we reach out to fulfill our yearnings for love, we may create deep bonds that last a lifetime.

The zodiacal sign of the progressed moon reveals how we can best nurture ourselves and others, and the house position shows the area of life where that nurturing can best take place. For example, in the sign of Gemini, we can nurture ourselves and others through reading, learning, and teaching. As it moves through the tenth house, we can actually find fulfillment by immersing ourselves in our careers and being a leader for others.

Opportunities to Make It Big!

Our career highs and lows can be understood when we look at transiting Jupiter, Saturn and the Midheaven. When Jupiter, the quintessential planet of opportunities, makes contact with our natal Sun, our dreams can come true! For those of us who have put in effort toward our goals, now is the time our ship may come in. We can experience progress in our careers when Jupiter makes a nice aspect to our Midheaven, and/or transits our tenth house. This is when we can experience the fruits of our labors in the form of more recognition, money, or career advancement. This is the area of our life where we want to "go for it," but we must be cautious of overextending ourselves.

Saturn, the planet of discipline, can lead to significant career advancements when it aspects our Midheaven or transits our tenth house. We may finally get the respect and status we seek, as we are seen as an expert authority in our area of work. Although this may come with added work and responsibilities, it is a gift for our career.

When our progressed Midheaven enters our eleventh house, our career usually takes off. Since this house deals with our life purpose, we have the opportunity to align our career with our mission. Some people may open a new business, or join with other like-minded people in some type of humanitarian organization.

If we want to know when the universe will "show us the money," we can follow the cycles of Saturn and Jupiter transiting through the houses to obtain this answer. The two houses that deal with money are the second and eighth houses. When Jupiter transits through the second house we might receive a raise at work, while in the eighth house it could be a hike in our stock portfolio or even an inheritance. The opposite effect may occur when Saturn transits these houses. In the second house it typically signals the need to tighten our purse strings and balance our budget. In the eighth house we may find our revenue that usually comes from other sources, such as a spouse, or interest on investments, is decreased or restricted in some way.

Travel and Education with Jupiter

If we wonder when we will finally be able to take that dream vacation, we can look at Jupiter and activity in our third and ninth houses. Jupiter is most often associated with travel, so when it transits either the third house or the ninth house, it can begin a cycle of domestic travel in the former house, or overseas travel in the latter house.

The ninth house relates to all activities that can broaden our horizons, so Jupiter or Saturn moving through this house can initiate a cycle of higher education or spiritual study. Saturn can help us get disciplined to get a bachelor's or master's degree, while Jupiter may inspire us to begin a course of spiritual study.

Change and Transformation with Uranus and Pluto

Uranus and Pluto are going to cause change and upheaval in whatever house they transit. Uranus brings unexpected change, and a desire for greater freedom. Uranus moving through our sixth or tenth house will often bring a job change. If we have been putting up with a controlling and negative boss, we may finally break free of this suffocation and become self-employed.

Pluto likes to stir the pot in the house it transits. This can take many forms, such as removing something from our life that is blocking our growth, or bringing us a challenging relationship that transforms us in some way. We can examine the house Pluto is transiting and notice how we have become overly obsessive or attached to a way of life. Next, we can find a way to redirect our energies by making a contribution to the world which gets the attention off ourselves and allows us to see the world in an expanded way. Pluto is a constant reminder that life is about change.

Changing Our Identity with the Progressed Sun

The Sun travels through the different zodiac signs and stays in each sign for a duration of thirty years. It moves one degree per year, and there are thirty degrees in each sign. Depending on the degree of the Sun in our chart, we can calculate when it will leave its natal position and move into the next zodiac sign. This is a major astrological event when the Sun changes signs on our natal chart. For example, suppose Mark was born with his Sun at fifteen degrees of Pisces. Since there are thirty degrees per sign, and the Sun moves one degree per year, we know that at age fifteen his Sun will progress into the next sign of Aries.

Since the Sun relates to our identity, when it progresses into a new zodiac sign, our manner of relating to the world and others changes significantly. In the above example, Mark would move from passivity (Pisces) to assertiveness (Aries). He would have the opportunity to integrate a sense of individuality, strength, and courage (Aries) into himself. Luckily the Sun moves slowly, giving us thirty years to incorporate the new energies into ourselves.

In conclusion, our lives progress through various cycles which are influenced by the planets. These planetary cycles are opportunities for us to learn, grow, and change. Each planet brings a different type of wake-up call which affects every area of our lives, from education to career and love. Through an understanding of the planetary cycles, we can prepare ourselves to take advantage of the opportunities and lessons they offer. The following activities will help us make the most of these cycles in our lives.

Activities

1. To prepare for Jupiter transits, you can study what sign and house it will move through this year on your natal chart. Next, write how you can take advantage of Jupiter's opportunities and abundance.

2. To prepare for a future Saturn return or transit, you can study the sign and house it will move through this year on your natal chart. Next, write down the lessons Saturn wants you to learn, and in what ways you can mature. Lastly, you can write a strategy for fulfilling your dreams.

3. To prepare for a future Uranus opposition or transit, you can study the sign and house Uranus will move through this year on your natal chart. Next, write about your unique essence and how you can contribute your gifts to the world. Lastly, write what is limiting you in this area of your life and how you can free yourself from these constraints.

4. To prepare for Neptune's wake-up calls, you can study the sign and house position Neptune will move through on your astrology chart. Next write how you can open up to your spirituality and avoid escapist tendencies in this area of life. Lastly, you can create disciplines and practices to connect with your higher self.

5. To prepare for Pluto's call to action, you can study the sign and house position Pluto will move through on your astrology chart. Next, write how you can use your power for transforming yourself and the world. Lastly, you can let go of what no longer serves you in this area of life.

6. You can benefit by visiting an astrologer for a comprehensive reading to determine when

opportunities for love, career advancement, travel, and education will affect your chart (readings offered at www.intuitiveschool. com).

Chapter 17
Success Stories

Make use of time, let not advantage slip.
—William Shakespeare

We have learned about the power of numerology and astrology to understand the timing in our lives. Now it's time to look at some real-life examples. I am sharing stories of people who had major life transformations and success in their lives that corresponded to significant astrological and numerological cycles.

Each person who shared their stories with me had worked many years before attaining success. They are proof that just because a beneficial astrological cycle is coming our way, if we haven't done our work, then we may not reap the benefits of the cycle. These people were willing to take the steps to achieve their dreams.

Some people are impatient and want to get to the top ladder without taking other steps, which can lead to many problems. Some people have the attitude "If I can't have the top-paying job now, then I'm just not going to work at all." They not only miss out on the joy of the baby steps, but they most likely will never get to taste success. Let's read about some people who had the courage to manifest their dreams!

The Doll Maker

Marty is a true Pisces with great artistic talent. She had been making various types of crafts and selling them at art fairs for seventeen years before her hobby turned into a big business. In the spring of 1986 Marty was at an art show in Denver. A sales representative passed by her booth and liked Marty's work. She told Marty to send her something original. Marty got home and put her talents to work and Attic Babies were born. Her dolls, made from tea-stained cloth, were a hit! After the sales rep received the sample doll, she placed an order for $160,000 of Attic Babies. This was the beginning of Marty's successful doll line, which would run until 2002. During this time Marty received many accolades, including small businessperson of the year in Oklahoma, and being chosen by the governor of Oklahoma to design a doll for the former first lady Barbara Bush. Her factory grew to employ over one hundred people. Let's now look at her numerology and astrology cycles to see how her success was supported by these influences.

In 1986 Marty was in a personal year 6 (her birthdate is February 25, 1951). A personal year 6 indicates the potential to advance in our career. It also coincided with the birth of her son, as women often have children in a year 6. Marty was in an essence number 3, a period about self-expression and creativity. During this essence number she advanced her career from crafting at home and selling at local fairs to becoming a world-renowned doll maker.

Astrologically there were many factors influencing her success. First, her progressed Sun was in Aries in the tenth house. She was born a Pisces, yet her success came when she had progressed into Aries. The strength, courage, and innovative qualities of Aries helped Marty launch her unique line of dolls. The passage of the Sun moving through the tenth house helped bring the focus to her career. Her Midheaven had recently moved into her eleventh house, allowing her to align her career with her life purpose. Marty's pervious years of hard work paid off, so when she received her first large order of $160,000, she was ready! Her ability to network and meet up with influential people was also helped by three other planets that had progressed into the eleventh house; Venus, Mercury, and Mars. Had Marty not been at that fair in Denver where she met the sales representative, she might not have had so much success. Her progressed Saturn in her fourth house shows the challenges and burdens she faced with trying to raise children and build her business at the same time.

Transiting Jupiter was in Marty's tenth house at the time she launched her Attic Babies. Jupiter was also in the sign of Pisces, highlighting artistic creativity. Furthermore, transiting Jupiter was conjunct (touching) her North Node. This triggered her purpose in life to be activated. Transiting Uranus was moving through her sixth house, signaling a change in her career.

A Spiritual Calling

Robin was working as a nurse when she had a powerful meditation experience where she received the message that she was to open a light center. She followed the message, and four years later she purchased thirty-five acres and an old barn. Today she happily manages her nature oasis that offers holistic workshops held in the renovated barn.

She has provided a sanctuary for those seeking healing in nature for over twenty-six years and recently added sixty more acres to her light center. Let's explore what numbers and planets were helping her to answer this calling to serve others.

Robin was in a personal year 8 when she took the plunge and bought the land in 1994. An 8 is a wonderful year to take advantage of business opportunities. It is also known as a harvest year, where all our efforts come to fruition. Robin had taken her retirement money from working many years in nursing to purchase the land. She was reaping what she had sown for many years.

Robin was in her Life Class number 5 when she started the Light Center. This number urges us to learn from our experiences rather than from books. The Light Center was definitely a hands-on experience for Robin as she learned to renovate an old barn, grow a garden, and work with the land. In addition, she needed to learn how to run a holistic center and deal with scheduling events, advertising, and working with all types of people. The 5 had shown her that experience was her best teacher.

Robin was also in an essence number 9. This period asks us to reach out and serve humanity. The mission of the center is in alignment with this number, "Holding sacred space for renewal, globally and locally, The Light Center serves individuals and families seeking wholeness in partnership with Nature." Since its inception, the Light Center has helped thousands of people heal and connect through nature and higher learning.

Robin was in a pinnacle 1 and a challenge 1 when the center came into being. The pinnacle period 1 showed the need for her to be independent, assertive, and courageous. The challenge #1 tested her to be brave and follow her beliefs and values. Even though people around her thought she was crazy to buy a property out in the country with a dilapidated barn, she listened to her heart and followed through.

The planets were also supporting Robin's new endeavor. Uranus was transiting her tenth house, signaling a change in direction in her career. She was also being inspired by Neptune transiting her tenth house to blend spirituality into her career. Venus, the Moon, and the Midheaven were transiting her ninth house, which emphasized her desire to answer the spiritual calling. Her South Node was also transiting her ninth house, which is where she was facing her past. Robin's wisdom, compassion, and spiritual understandings have been built over many lifetimes, as revealed by her natal South Node in the ninth house. The progressed South Node came along to remind her of her spiritual wisdom and the need for her to share it with the world.

In 1994 when Robin purchased the property, she

had the transiting Sun, Pluto, Mercury, Jupiter, and North Node all in the eighth house. This house of transformation revealed that Robin was in for a major growth spurt. Robin had to face many of her fears as she embarked on this venture. The eighth house requires us to face our fears and dark sides and overcome them in order to cause transformation.

Building Spiritual Community

Gail had been involved in metaphysical study for many years. She was seeking a way to live in alignment with her beliefs with other like-minded people and a place where her two children could learn spiritual principals. Some friends were building a spiritual community, and they invited Gail and her husband to be a part of it. Gail and her family decided to leave behind suburbia for the country where they hoped to build a deeper spiritual connection. Let's see how the cycles of her life moved her through this journey that was full of unexpected twists and turns.

In 1995 Gail and her husband purchased a farm in this spiritual community, which was a personal year 5 for her, based on her birthdate of July 1, 1956. A 5 year is about change and adventure which requires adaptability. This suburban wife with two kids had to make many changes in her lifestyle, including removing her kids from public school and homeschooling them. She had to change her daily life to align with the activities, spiritual practices, and expectations of the community. Gail took the opportunity to completely change her life with the energy of her 5 personal year.

Gail was in a life class 1. This life class is about learning to be independent and not following the crowd. Gail's decision to move to this community was an unconventional life choice that required her to follow her instincts rather than what was socially acceptable. This is a period where we can move toward fulfilling our life mission. Gail had been interested in metaphysics for many years and had a dream of creating a lifestyle centered around her spiritual beliefs. The community was the answer to her desire.

Gail was in an essence number 9 period. When she joined the community, it allowed her to take full advantage of this period of mental and spiritual expansion. Gail served others by teaching the kids in the community.

The main event Gail was going through astrologically during her time in the community was her Uranian opposition. This is a period in life where we are urged to follow our unique path and fulfill the purpose of our Uranian influence. Gail has her natal Uranus in her ninth house of spirituality and higher education. Gail was never interested in following a traditional religion, rather she was drawn to the mystical sciences. The community she joined was a group of people with a unique mission to live like Christ and in alignment with the Universal Laws and Truths.

Embracing New Beginnings

Sophie's life was profoundly affected by her essence numbers. When she turned twenty-four, she was under the influence of essence number 1 until the age of twenty-eight. Sophie did all the things this essence number urges us to do; begin new projects, be brave, and go after our dreams. At twenty-four she finished nursing school and accepted a job at a nearby hospital. A year later she got married, and the following year she had a baby. I believe her success is due to her willingness to take advantage of the many opportunities that presented themselves with the 1 energy.

When she began her first Saturn return, Sophie decided to take her career to the next level. She returned to college to pursue a master's degree to become a certified nurse practitioner. She also had another child, and she purchased a larger home. Like many people, Sophie has not been immune from the struggles to attain all her goals during her Saturn return. The demands of her nursing job, attending school and clinical trainings, and raising children filled her plate.

Since she answered Saturn's call to be disciplined, she is now reaping the rewards. Her master's degree allowed her to transition from twelve-hour days as a floor nurse to a nine-to-five position where she is able to treat patients without the restrictive hospital policies and work less hours for more pay. She now enjoys more time with her husband and four children. Sophie is an example of the rewards that come from taking on new challenges and being disciplined.

The folks in this chapter are testimony to the beneficial results we can obtain when we use the planetary and numerological cycles to our benefit. Although they do not dictate our lives, they can reveal potential opportunities and challenges. It is up to each one of us to make choices in alignment with our soul desires. As Napoleon Hill once said, "What the mind can conceive and believe it can achieve."

Let's become the masters of timing in our lives by completing the following activity.

Activity: Destiny Cycles

1. Make a timeline of significant events in your

life. Include both the positive and challenging events. Next, look at the astrological and numerological cycles occurring at those times. What conclusions can you draw?

Chapter 18

Our Time Has Come to an End

The only reason for time is so that everything
doesn't happen at once.

—Albert Einstein

By now you may be wondering if everything is actually happening simultaneously, and in order for us to make sense of it all, time has broken up our life events into digestible bites.

We are spiritual beings with the ability to go beyond the constraints of time. Our exploration of time has revealed that it is different depending on if we look at it through our spiritual or physical eyes. The great paradox of time is that on the physical level it exists and yet on the spiritual level it doesn't exist.

Life gets really interesting when we use tools to transcend the limitations of time such as breathwork and meditation. The simple act of creating in a joyful space can help us forget that time exists.

This book reminds us once again of the importance of working on ourselves. If we want to manifest "stuff" the first place to begin is with ourselves.

Visualization and intuition are two abilities that can help our mind navigate the constraints of time. Visualization is a faculty of our subconscious mind and allows us to quicken our manifestations by allowing our mind to do most of the work. Our intuition saves us time by showing us exactly what we should be doing. If we listen, we can avoid delays and interruptions that we are not aware of consciously. Our intuition can see beyond the constraints of the conscious mind. For example, our conscious mind can't see a road blockage miles down the road, but the subconscious can, and will be able to warn us about it through our intuition.

The unseen universal laws can help or hinder us, depending on how we use them. One such law, known as the law of cause and effect (karma), can speed up or slow down our rate of evolution. If we don't learn our lessons, we slow ourselves down by repeating the same lessons over and over again. However, if we recognize the effects we create, we can repeat the actions that cause the effects we want, while ceasing the actions that cause the effects we dislike.

Service-oriented people are the fuel of society. They get things rolling! If things aren't manifesting for us, we can help someone else and get out of our own way! We'll not only gain the satisfaction of knowing we improved the life of someone else, but we'll fill up our spiritual bank account so we can make a withdrawal when we need it.

Slow is the new fast when it comes to understanding how to manifest quickly. One way to slow down is to properly prepare a foundation which creates a space for us to receive our creation. Nature is a constant reminder of the need to go with the flow. Each season prepares us for the next one and lays the foundation for success.

We are often thrown off balance when an event occurs out of the sequence we imagined. However, these so-called misplaced events are actually gifts that will help us in ways we often don't see at the time they occur.

Two amazing tools to help us relieve the ambiguity of when things will happen are astrology and numerology. Each one of these intuitive sciences offers some ways to penetrate future possibilities. Numerology uses numbers and their vibrational meanings to show us when and what events are in our realm of possibility. Astrology guides us by using planetary movements as an indicator of potentials. The planets remind us that life is about cycles and timing, and understanding our individual cycles is the key to greater success in manifesting our desires.

I hope that this book can help us change the tendency to use time as a constraint or limitation. Time is precious and can work to our benefit if we understand and work in accordance with the various cycles. Although time is a "real" structure in the physical sense, our eyes are now open to the possibility that we can transcend it until one day we will return to our true spiritual essence,

which is timeless and eternal.

Carpe Diem

About the Author

Kathryn Andries has been teaching self-development techniques and coaching individuals to discover their passion and purpose in life for over 20 years.

She is the co-founder of Intuitive School, which offers a variety of metaphysical classes and readings. She and her husband Patrick are the hosts of "Spirits Journey" radio where they offer spiritual solutions for everyday living.

After obtaining a Bachelor of Arts degree from the University of Michigan, Kathryn didn't feel it would help her fulfill her true purpose in life. This led her to study holistic health at Body Mind College in California, and later went on to complete extensive studies in the intuitive arts at the Berkeley Psychic Institute, the School of Metaphysics, and the American Federation of Astrologers.

Kathryn has authored five other books on the topics of life purpose, relationships, dreams and visualization.

Books by Kathryn Andries

Soul Choices
Published by: Ozark Mountain Publishing

Soul Choices Workbook
Published by: Ozark Mountain Publishing

Soul Choices Relationships
Published by: Ozark Mountain Publishing

Dream Doctor
Published by: Ozark Mountain Publishing

Naked in Public
Published by: Ozark Mountain Publishing

The Big Desire
Published by: Ozark Mountain Publishing

For more information about any of the above titles, soon to be released titles,
or other items in our catalog, write, phone or visit our website:
Ozark Mountain Publishing, Inc.
PO Box 754, Huntsville, AR 72740
479-738-2348/800-935-0045
www.ozarkmt.com

Other Books by Ozark Mountain Publishing, Inc.

Dolores Cannon
A Soul Remembers Hiroshima
Between Death and Life
Conversations with Nostradamus,
    Volume I, II, III
The Convoluted Universe -Book One,
    Two, Three, Four, Five
The Custodians
Five Lives Remembered
Jesus and the Essenes
Keepers of the Garden
Legacy from the Stars
The Legend of Starcrash
The Search for Hidden Sacred
    Knowledge
They Walked with Jesus
The Three Waves of Volunteers and
    the New Earth
A Vey Special Friend
Aron Abrahamsen
Holiday in Heaven
James Ream Adams
Little Steps
Justine Alessi & M. E. McMillan
Rebirth of the Oracle
Kathryn Andries
Time: The Second Secret
Cat Baldwin
Divine Gifts of Healing
The Forgiveness Workshop
Penny Barron
The Oracle of UR
P.E. Berg & Amanda Hemmingsen
The Birthmark Scar
Dan Bird
Finding Your Way in the Spiritual Age
Waking Up in the Spiritual Age
Julia Cannon
Soul Speak – The Language of Your
    Body
Ronald Chapman
Seeing True

Jack Churchward
Lifting the Veil on the Lost
    Continent of Mu
The Stone Tablets of Mu
Patrick De Haan
The Alien Handbook
Paulinne Delcour-Min
Spiritual Gold
Holly Ice
Divine Fire
Joanne DiMaggio
Edgar Cayce and the Unfulfilled
    Destiny of Thomas Jefferson
    Reborn
Anthony DeNino
The Power of Giving and Gratitude
Carolyn Greer Daly
Opening to Fullness of Spirit
Anita Holmes
Twidders
Aaron Hoopes
Reconnecting to the Earth
Patricia Irvine
In Light and In Shade
Kevin Killen
Ghosts and Me
Donna Lynn
From Fear to Love
Curt Melliger
Heaven Here on Earth
Where the Weeds Grow
Henry Michaelson
And Jesus Said – A Conversation
Andy Myers
Not Your Average Angel Book
Guy Needler
Avoiding Karma
Beyond the Source – Book 1, Book 2
The History of God
The Origin Speaks

For more information about any of the above titles, soon to be released titles,
or other items in our catalog, write, phone or visit our website:
PO Box 754, Huntsville, AR 72740|479-738-2348/800-935-0045|www.ozarkmt.com

Other Books by Ozark Mountain Publishing, Inc.

The Anne Dialogues
The Curators
Psycho Spiritual Healing
James Nussbaumer
And Then I Knew My Abundance
The Master of Everything
Mastering Your Own Spiritual
    Freedom
Living Your Dram, Not Someone Else's
Sherry O'Brian
Peaks and Valley's
Gabrielle Orr
Akashic Records: One True Love
Let Miracles Happen
Nikki Pattillo
Children of the Stars
A Golden Compass
Victoria Pendragon
Sleep Magic
The Sleeping Phoenix
Being In A Body
Alexander Quinn
Starseeds What's It All About
Charmian Redwood
A New Earth Rising
Coming Home to Lemuria
Richard Rowe
Imagining the Unimaginable
Exploring the Divine Library
Garnet Schulhauser
Dancing on a Stamp
Dancing Forever with Spirit
Dance of Heavenly Bliss
Dance of Eternal Rapture
Dancing with Angels in Heaven
Manuella Stoerzer
Headless Chicken
Annie Stillwater Gray
Education of a Guardian Angel
The Dawn Book
Work of a Guardian Angel

Joys of a Guardian Angel
Blair Styra
Don't Change the Channel
Who Catharted
Natalie Sudman
Application of Impossible Things
L.R. Sumpter
Judy's Story
The Old is New
We Are the Creators
Artur Tradevosyan
Croton
Croton II
Jim Thomas
Tales from the Trance
Jolene and Jason Tierney
A Quest of Transcendence
Paul Travers
Dancing with the Mountains
Nicholas Vesey
Living the Life-Force
Dennis Wheatley/ Maria Wheatley
The Essential Dowsing Guide
Maria Wheatley
Druidic Soul Star Astrology
Sherry Wilde
The Forgotten Promise
Lyn Willmott
A Small Book of Comfort
Beyond all Boundaries Book 1
Beyond all Boundaries Book 2
Beyond all Boundaries Book 3
Stuart Wilson & Joanna Prentis
Atlantis and the New Consciousness
Beyond Limitations
The Essenes -Children of the Light
The Magdalene Version
Power of the Magdalene
Sally Wolf
Life of a Military Psychologist

For more information about any of the above titles, soon to be released titles,
or other items in our catalog, write, phone or visit our website:
PO Box 754, Huntsville, AR 72740|479-738-2348/800-935-0045|www.ozarkmt.com